RALEGH'S LOST COLONY

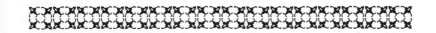

Ralegh's Lost Colony

David N. Durant

ATHENEUM   NEW YORK

1981

Library of Congress Cataloging in Publication Data

Durant, David N.
    Ralegh's lost colony.

    Bibliography: p.
    Includes index
    1. Roanoke Island—History. 2. Raleigh's Roanoke
colonies, 1584-1590. 3. Raleigh, Walter, Sir, 1552?-
1618. I. Title.
F262.R4D87   1981   975.6'175   80-65992
    ISBN 0-689-11098-7

To all my many American friends and relatives.
Also to the Alumni of the Attingham Summer School.
This narrative is a reminder of our shared heritage.

Contents

Illustrations

The author and publishers would like to thank the following for permission to use pictures: the Trustees of the British Museum for 1–9 and 15; the National Park Service, USA, for 10; the Public Record Office (Crown copyright) for 11; and the National Portrait Gallery for 12, 13, and 14.

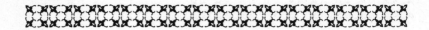

Maps

Preface

This narrative account of Ralegh's lost colony could not have been written in this form without the immense and valuable research of Professor D. B. Quinn, published as *The Roanoke Voyages* in two volumes by the Hakluyt Society, in 1955. I am also indebted to his *England and the Discovery of America* (1974) for many points in the reconstruction of the fate of the lost colony. Since then little new has been discovered about the fascinating story of the first English colony in America. My own research convinces me that Ralph Lane's fort cannot have been the present Fort Raleigh National Historic Site at Roanoke Island, North Carolina. I firmly believe that the site of the fort and the settlement must be looked for elsewhere. This decade will see the celebration of the 400th anniversary of this first English colony in America and it would be as good a time as any to search for and excavate that first settlement. Only when this is discovered shall we be able to add anything substantial to what we already know about this exciting chapter of the common history of our two countries.

I have used endnotes sparingly mainly due to the availability of Professor Quinn's *The Roanoke Voyages*, and the enquiring reader will easily find in his work the references to the facts I quote. However, when I have used a different source this is made clear in the notes. Indian personal names are strange to those used to reading English and, to avoid confusing the reader, I have attempted rough translations of their meanings based on the short list of Algonkian words compiled by the Rev. James A. Geary in *The Roanoke Voyages*, Appendix 11.

From the age of thirty, Sir Walter Raleigh spelt his surname 'Ralegh', and I have therefore used this spelling throughout.

I suppose it would be too much to hope that the legends that Ralegh introduced tobacco and brought the potato to England from Virginia will from now be regarded as incorrect. Ralegh and his men introduced the clay pipe to England, and not tobacco; and the potato, wherever it came from, was not from Virginia – it is not native to that part of America.

Gene and Charlotte Brown of Raleigh, North Carolina, USA, are two great friends and I must thank them for taking me off for two days to Roanoke Island. It is doubtful if I should ever have got there but for their kindness and hospitality. My thanks are again due to my wife, Christabel, for typing the revised manuscript, to Dorothy Gwynn for typing the final manuscript, and to Barbara Gough in London and Barbara Anderman in New York for their valuable and much appreciated editing.

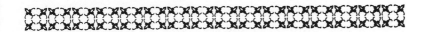

Chronology

1578

11 June	Sir Humphrey Gilbert granted patent of discovery.
26 September	Ralegh's first command in the *Falcon*.

1583

29 August	Sir Humphrey Gilbert drowned in the *Squirrel*.

1584

25 March	Walter Ralegh granted patent of discovery.
27 April	Philip Amadas and Arthur Barlow sail in two ships on reconnaissance of North America.
13 July	Formal ceremony of possession, in Queen Elizabeth's name, of what is now North Carolina; ceremony is held on what is now Bodie Island, near Roanoke Island, in the Carolina Outer Banks.
August	The two barks leave for England. Amadas stopping off in Chesapeake Bay is met by hostile Indians.
Mid-September	Return to England with two Indians: Wanchese and Manteo.

1585

6 January	Walter Ralegh knighted and permitted to call his colony Virginia.
9 April	Sir Richard Grenville sails for Virginia with seven vessels and 100 colonists.
20 June	Florida coast sighted.
28 June	The *Tiger* nearly wrecked two days after arriving off Wococon Island.
5 August	John Arundell sails for England.
17 August	Fort completed. Ralph Lane appointed Governor of colony of 107 men.

25 August	Sir Richard Grenville sails for England in the *Tiger*; arrives 18 October.
October	Explorations carried out in Virginia. Party spends winter in Chesapeake Bay.

1586

March	Indians begin to resent English colonists. Lane ambushed while on expedition up Albemarle River.
April/May	Sir Richard Grenville sails with eight relief ships from Bideford.
10 June	Lane makes surprise attack on Indians after learning of plan to attack the colony.
8 June	Sir Francis Drake sighted off Croatoan Island.
10 June	Drake and his fleet anchor off Port Ferdinando. He offers ship and crew with stores to enable Lane to finish exploration before returning to England. Plan agreed until hurricane on 13 June.
16 June	Drake loses four ships in severe storm including that intended for Lane. Colonists decide to return to England with Drake.
June	Single supply ship arrives to find settlement deserted.
August	Sir Richard Grenville arrives with seven ships and relief stores. Finds settlement deserted and leaves fifteen 'caretaker' colonists.
September/ October	Caretaker colonists attacked by Indians, two killed and the rest never heard of again.

1587

7 January	Grant of arms for 'Cittie of Ralegh', appointing John White as Governor and thirteen assistants to establish the 'Cittie' in Chesapeake Bay.
8 May	Three ships carrying 115 colonists – including seventeen women, two of them pregnant, and nine children – sail from Plymouth.
22 July	Ships arrive off Port Ferdinando intending to pick up caretaker colonists before going on to Chesapeake. The pilot, Fernandez, disregards Ralegh's instructions and leaves all the colonists at Roanoke Island.
13 August	Manteo baptised and created Lord of Roanoke under Sir Walter Ralegh.

18 August	John White's daughter, Elenor Dare, gives birth to daughter, Virginia and has her baptised.
22 August	Colonists insist that John White should leave for England to arrange essential supplies.
27 August	White leaves in the fly-boat for England. Colonists intend moving to new site.
16 October	White reaches Ireland after troublesome voyage; transfers to a ship for England.
8 November	White arrives in England.
20 November	White urges Ralegh to send immediate supplies to colony. Ships fail to sail.

1588

February	Account of the resources and potential of a Virginian colony published by Thomas Hariot in *A Briefe and True Report*.
End March	Grenville ready to sail for Virginia with relief stores in eight ships. Privy Council order Grenville to join Drake at Plymouth in Armada emergency.
22 April	John White manages to sail for Virginia in two ships with eleven colonists: seven men and four women.
22 May	White returns to England, having been attacked and looted; Virginia never reached.
28 May	Spanish *barca luenga* finds slipway at Port Ferdinando.

1589

7 March	A holding company formed for the 'Cittie of Ralegh' venture to relieve the colonists, includes Richard Hakluyt and London merchants. No relief expedition leaves England.
December possibly Jan. (1590)	Richard Hakluyt publishes *Principal navigations*, giving account of Virginian colony, 1584–8.

1590

20 March	John White sails in the *Hopewell*, which takes him to Roanoke Island on the return from a privateering venture in the Caribbean.
May	The *Moonlight*, belonging to William Sanderson, investor in the 1589 Virginian venture, sails for Roanoke Island with stores for the colonists.

May   Theodor de Bry publishes *America* with Hariot's *Briefe and True Report*, giving account of Virginian colony 1585–6 with engravings after John White's drawings.

15 August   The *Hopewell* brings John White to Port Ferdinando. White finds settlement on Roanoke Island deserted. A message on a tree leads White to think the colony has moved to Croatoan Island but bad weather prevents him making a visit there. Weather forces them to return to England.

24 October   White, in the *Hopewell*, reaches Plymouth.

1591 (or after)
John White settles in Newtown, Kilmore, Co. Cork.

1593
4 February   John White writes to Richard Hakluyt from Newtown, Ireland.

1595
Raleigh, returning from Guiana, fails to put into Roanoke Island or Chesapeake.

1602
March   Samuel Mace, said to have been to 'Virginia twice before' sent by Ralegh to collect plants from area south of Carolina Outer Banks.

1603
24 March   Queen Elizabeth dies, James I proclaimed King.

15 July   Sir Walter Ralegh arrested for treason.

5 September   Three 'Virginians' paddle a canoe in front of Cecil's house on Thames.

1604
Mid-Summer Terms of Peace Treaty with Spain agreed in London on lines which indicate belief in survival of Virginian colony.

1604 or 1605
English ship sails into Chesapeake and kidnaps three Indians.

1605

September   Play by Ben Jonson and others Eastward Ho.
End of April Slaughter of lost colonists at Chesapeake by
              Powhatan.

1608

January   Jamestown colonists send a search party to seek the
              lost colonists; some are rumoured to be still living.
              Survivors not found.

1609

Early in   Jamestown colonists send a man with two Indian
the year   guides to search for seven lost colonists rumoured
              living on Chowan River. Survivors not found. This is
              followed by a second search party sent inland. No
              survivors found.

PART ONE

The First Colony

 1

'Neere to Heaven by Sea as by Land'

Through the clearing battle-smoke Captain Walter Ralegh could see that things had gone badly for him. Now that the cannons had stopped firing, the cries and screams of the wounded and dying could be heard. In the slow, heaving swell the small ships rolled, and running blood made bizarre patterns across the wooden decks – littered with debris from the shattered rigging. Ralegh's small fleet was battered and disabled. His own ship, the *Falcon*, was probably most battered of all. And there was nothing to show for it: no rich prizes, no priceless cargoes, no valuable hostages and no victory or glory.

As the Spanish ships disappeared over the horizon, the survivors, tired by the excitement and strain of the fight, began to set their small ships to rights making them seaworthy for the voyage back to England. Shot-through rigging had to be cut adrift; hulls damaged by Spanish cannons made weather-tight; the mess of battle cleared from the decks; the blood washed away; the injured attended to and the dead given a quick sea burial. This small unresolved sea fight in the year 1579 was of no consequence and is almost unrecorded. Like the dead, it would have been forgotten had it not been provoked by Walter Ralegh.

The *Falcon*, young Walter Ralegh's first command (he was only twenty-four) was a ship of 100 tons. Although heavily armed with '15 cast peces, four fowlers, 12 double bases', she was no match against a heavier broadside. The fight had been an occasion when prudence would have been better than honour or glory. But that was not in Ralegh's character. Furthermore the *Falcon* represented the Queen's investment in the expedition. There would be some explaining to do: a profitless venture and a damaged ship added up to a royal loss.

This minor engagement marked the end of a disastrous venture organised by Ralegh's half-brother, Sir Humphrey Gilbert. Gilbert had intended to sail from Plymouth in September 1578 in command of a fleet of eleven ships and 500 men, to explore the coast of America in preparation for a colonising expedition, by a patent granted to him by Queen Elizabeth in June that year. From the start nothing had gone right. Four of the ships had sailed from Plymouth to go pirating against Spanish shipping in the Bay of Biscay abandoning the main purpose of the venture. The remaining seven, when they could get away, were driven back by gales. Their second attempt was no better and storms scattered the fleet leaving only Ralegh, in the *Falcon*, accompanied by one, or at most two, ships to keep to the original plan. Shortage of cash was the main cause of the problems Gilbert was encountering, and shortage of cash, too, caused Ralegh's ship to be ill-provisioned. Shortage of food forced him to turn back to England and, in returning, near the Cape Verde Islands he met the superior force of the Spanish. This one-sided engagement was Ralegh's first experience of the hazards of colonising. It did not deter him.

In late May 1579, Ralegh, in the *Falcon*, limped into the shelter of Dartmouth roads with the dream of an American colony no further advanced. What Ralegh thought about this minor set-back we do not know, he probably brushed it aside as a lesson learnt, and looked forward to better success. Neither do we know how he was received by the Queen when he came to make his report on the voyage which had brought no return but a badly damaged ship. His case would have been supported by Walsingham, the influential Secretary of State, but apart from him he had no important friends at court; in 1579 he was unknown at the centre of power.

Ralegh, however, had strong personal assets. Gifted with great charm – when he cared to use it – he was also strikingly good-looking, slender and wiry and over six feet tall. In that dazzling, but essentially middle-aged, Elizabethan court circle he was not easily overlooked as a young man. We know his appearance from the Hilliard miniature now in the National Portrait Gallery, London. Dated by dress as around 1585, it is the earliest likeness to have survived. Ralegh's face, with a trim, pointed beard, shows a purposeful, dashing expression, a slight smile playing beneath an upswept, brown moustache. His curling, brown hair is brushed back and ornamented with double rows of pearls, and grey eyes stare back at us, seeming to mock, posing a question he knows we cannot answer.

In his early years, before he gained the Queen's favour, Ralegh was always hard up. The reason is not difficult to find. Acquisitive, like all Raleghs, Walter was flamboyant and consequently extravagant whether he had money or not. Like an actor, he needed an audience, and his life was constantly played for the limelight. And it was limelight that Ralegh had been seeking when he attacked the superior Spanish ships. No doubt he was spurred on to redoubled effort by the excitement of the engagement, thinking that if he came out of it badly then he could talk his way out of trouble later. Vastly self-confident he was also self-destructively proud. His moods alternated between high elation and deep depression – the temperament of a manic depressive – and at times he displayed an almost neurotic hysteria. Ralegh was a genius with all the allied imbalance of character.

Whatever reception Ralegh and Gilbert had at court after their abortive expedition, it was fortuitous for both of them that a more pressing need than overseas settlement was occupying the urgent attention of Elizabeth and her privy council. Ireland, once more, was in revolt. For Ralegh and Gilbert this was perhaps as well. Gilbert was under a cloud because he had permitted part of his fleet to go pirating, and Ralegh, if he had been forgiven by the Queen, was soon in trouble. He was briefly imprisoned twice for that damnable pride of his, serving one week in the Fleet for fighting a duel, and then in the Marshalsea for fighting on the tennis court at Whitehall! Both Ralegh and Gilbert were involved with the army in Ireland, and America was put out of mind for a time.

However Gilbert's patent lasted only for six years and by 1580 time was running out. If a colony was to be established, then an early exploration of possible sites was an urgent priority. Raising money by assigning lands he had not yet discovered, Gilbert was able to equip his own small frigate, the *Squirrel*, to cross the Atlantic under a Portuguese pilot, Simon Fernandez. Fernandez was undoubtedly the best man for the venture to be found in England. He had sailed with Ralegh in the *Falcon* and the two had reached some sort of amity and understanding of each other.

He was also referred to as 'Master Secretary Walsingham's man'. It is likely that he was chosen for the *Squirrel* not only to pilot the vessel, but to provide first-hand details of Spanish America to Walsingham.

Fernandez had arrived in England in about .1573 with an abiding hatred of the Spanish. (One would love to know more of this man but his early history is unrecorded.) He had considerable experience of sailing the West Indies and the American coast, but liked nothing so much as robbing Spanish shipping. If there was no Spanish shipping, he had no scruples about taking other nations' vessels. Had England been officially at war with Spain, Fernandez' private vendetta would have been an advantage to his adopted country; as it was, his pillaging of foreign shipping was an embarrassment. He had a forceful personality, was distrusted by many and quarrelled with his shipmates – all of which contributed to the failure of his last American expedition. His value was his unrivalled knowledge of the American Atlantic Coast.

To assure Fernandez' good behaviour, Gilbert had to enter into a bond for £500. Even in so tiny a vessel as the *Squirrel*, with only about eleven on board, the privy council were taking no chances; they knew Fernandez' reputation and they remembered the last expedition Gilbert had enterprised.

The *Squirrel* left Dartmouth before the end of March 1580 and, making a fast crossing, landed on an unspecified coast, returning before the end of June. The speed of this voyage demonstrates Fernandez' skill as a pilot, and the crossing would surely rank as a major seafaring achievement if we knew more about it. All that can be said is that contact was made with Indians who lived in houses 'buylt in Lyke mannor rounde', and that Fernandez' party brought back with them hides of what they called a hairy ox but which must have been bison.[2] No doubt Fernandez passed on to Gilbert and Walsingham all he had seen and discovered.

On 20 November that year, Fernandez paid a visit to Dr John Dee in Mortlake. Dee was a scientist, geographer and astrologer. As two of these skills bordered on the occult he was sometimes regarded by the uninformed as a charlatan, impostor and dabbler in black magic and consequently persecuted from time to time. He had been consulted by Gilbert in May 1577.[3] In fact almost all expeditions felt themselves ill equipped if they had not taken the latest advice from the great magus, Dr John Dee. In August 1580, Gilbert had assigned to Dee at his request most of what is now Canada, probably in return for his help. On the occasion of his visit to Dee in November Fernandez took a chart with him which he left for Dee to copy. This copy still exists and is based on a Spanish world map long outdated by 1580! What sort of game was Fernandez playing with the old man? For it is certain that Fernandez could never have made a record-breaking crossing of the Atlantic with such a chart since the latitudes are incorrect. It may be that he jealously guarded his own hard-won maps and had no intention of letting the detail become public property. We can be certain that Dee was told only as much about America as Fernandez chose to tell him.

It was not until the spring of 1582 that Gilbert started preparing for the great step into the New World. It may have been lack of funds which was holding him back. He had pleaded poverty to Walsingham in 1581,[4] but as he was only trying to get from his patron what was owing to him from the Irish expedition his cries should not be taken too literally. One often gains the impression of Walsingham craftily manipulating people for the benefit of England, and it may be that the director of Elizabethan secret strategy, feeling that it was not yet time for Gilbert's great venture, was holding him in check.

In May 1582 there was a fanfare of adroit propaganda when *Divers voyages*, a history of the discovery of America, was published by the younger Richard Hakluyt. Using this as a prospectus, Gilbert was able to sell vast areas of undiscovered land to speculators. In eight months from June 1582 Gilbert sold eight and a-half million acres to Catholics – which must have had Walsingham's blessing as Catholics on the other side of the Atlantic would cause no trouble in England. Even with this infusion of funds the expedition was still delayed by lack of money; then, in February 1583, Elizabeth, in one of her unpredictable gestures, forbade Ralegh and Gilbert to sail with their own expedition. But typically, partly relenting, at the last minute she permitted Gilbert alone to sail on the hazardous voyage. On 11 June, before the Queen could change her mind again, his fleet of five small ships and about 260 men left England.

This was an unlucky enterprise. Within days the largest vessel, the *Bark Ralegh* of 200 tons returned to Plymouth for lack of supplies – an indication of Gilbert's shortage of funds. The smallest ships, the *Swallow* and the tiny *Squirrel* of only ten tons, were lost in fog and only reunited with the *Delight*, Gilbert's command, and the *Golden Hind* off Newfoundland on 3 August. There the cod fishermen and merchants of mixed nationalities were amazed and no doubt unconcerned when Gilbert took possession of St John's and 200 leagues in each direction in the name of the Queen of England. This meaningless gesture was the only positive achievement of the whole unlucky expedition. Illness struck the crews of all four ships, no doubt due to bad rations and insufficient supplies, many died and others deserted. But Gilbert, undeterred shipped the sick back to England in the *Swallow* and set about exploring the coast southward with the three remaining vessels.

On 29 August bad luck struck them again, the *Delight*, with 100 men aboard, ground onto a shoal and sank as the others watched helplessly. The fault was Gilbert's, since he had refused to take notice of his pilot's advice. For the crew, enough was enough. When bad luck is a shipmate, there is only one course open – to end the voyage and pay off all hands. Gilbert was forced to head back for England by a disenchanted and near mutinous crew.

One of Gilbert's characteristics was an inborn obstinacy, and, when bad weather blew up on the return voyage, he refused to transfer from the *Squirrel* to the greater safety of the larger *Golden Hind*. The account of Gilbert's end must be apocryphal but it is worth re-telling. On his tiny ten-ton frigate in the blast of the storm Gilbert was seen to be:

sitting abaft with a booke in his hand, cried out to us in the *Hind* (so oft as we did approach within hearing). We are as neere to heaven by sea as by land. Reiterating the same speech, well beseeming a souldier, resolute in Jesus Christ, as I can testifie he was.[5]

That same night the lights of the little ship suddenly disappeared: 'For in that moment, the Frigate was devoured and swallowed up of the Sea.' It is a splendid story of the death of a hero but the detail is unlikely. Anyone who has been in a howling Atlantic gale will know that the roaring of the sea and the screaming of the wind make conversation on board difficult and it would have been impossible to hear someone calling from another ship. To sit abaft in a storm in so small a bobbing boat would also have been impossible – Gilbert would have been thrown or swept overboard. And to put another vessel as close as the account suggests would have been dangerous, foolhardy and inadvisable. Let us leave the account as a splendid story, but an imaginary one, and let Humphrey Gilbert rest in peace.

2

'Heathen and Barbarous Landes'

With the return to the West Country of the remains of Gilbert's second attempt to make a bridgehead in the New World it was a time for adding up losses. Gilbert's abortive venture in 1578 had not even crossed the Atlantic. Fernandez' remarkably swift voyage in the *Squirrel* in 1580 had been a reconnaissance. In the final attempt Gilbert's venture in 1582 had at least reached the coast of America but had achieved nothing. For so much to-ing and fro-ing, for so much money raised in worthless grants of land and spent, and for so many lives lost the result had been negligible. All there was to show for this considerable effort were some bison hides. And the inspiration behind it all, Gilbert, was now dead.

Ralegh had, at least, recovered his ship, the *Bark Ralegh,* and by the spring of 1584 had ceased mourning his half-brother's death and was once more bounding with confidence. His past deeds quite forgiven, he was basking in the rewarding light of the Queen's favour. He was also awarded letters patent to continue Gilbert's plan to establish a colony in America. In March of that year, Walter Ralegh, then junior knight for Devonshire in the House of Commons, formally asked his fellow members to confirm his patent to 'discover search fynde out and view such remote heathen and barbarous landes Countries and territories not actually possessed of any Christian Prynce'. Except for New-foundland, annexed by Gilbert on his last unlucky voyage, Ralegh now had full rights to take what he wished of undiscovered America and, like Gilbert, he had six years to found a permanent colony or his patent would be void. He lost no time.

Before anything else could be decided a site for the colony had to be discovered by means of a reconnaissance of the coast. Fernandez had made his epic voyage and brought back bison hides indicating that he had reached a northern destination but

Ralegh was barred from Newfoundland and the 200 leagues
south of it – to about Portland, Maine, on a modern map; and
the Spanish and French in Florida constricted his exploration to
the south. With good reason Ralegh took advice which
recommended a Mediterranean latitude of around thirty-five
degrees, the area of North Carolina.

Even whilst the ink was drying on his new patent, Ralegh's
preparations were in hand. On 27 April 1584 two vessels left the
West Country for the first part of his grand scheme of discovery
and colonisation. The information for this voyage is meagre. Two
ships probably sailed from Plymouth, slipping out at the time of
high water at the new moon, and high water at Plymouth that
day was approximately 4.30 in the morning and afternoon. Even
the names of the two vessels are not known for certain, but the
expedition was very much Ralegh's affair. The leader, or
admiral, Philip Amadas, was a member of Ralegh's household
and possibly sailed in Ralegh's *Bark Ralegh* of 200 tons' burden
with the indispensable Fernandez as master and pilot. The second
vessel, a pinnace, possibly also Ralegh's, was commanded by
Arthur Barlow who had been with Ralegh in Ireland in 1580.
Ralegh was not on either ship: Elizabeth had forbidden it again.

From England the two vessels took the usual West Indian
route, carried from the Canaries by the north-east trade winds.
Flying fish leapt out of the waves and, skimming the top of the
water, pointed the way. The ships arrived in the Caribbean by
way of the Dominican passage, briefly landing at Puerto Rico to
refill water casks and take on fresh food, and then making their
course northwards for the Florida Channel. Fernandez'
navigation had not been perfect. He had miscalculated the
current running from the Gulf of Mexico and was carried too far
to the east, toward the Bahamas, but it put the ships in no danger.
And on 2 July 1584 Arthur Barlow noted, 'we found schole
water, which smelt so sweetely and was so strong a smell, as if we
had been in the midst of some delicate garden, abounding with
all kinds of odoriferous flowers, by which we were assured that
land could not be farre distant'. After weeks at sea, breathing
only clear sea wind flavoured with salt spray, the sense of smell is
sharpened and the warm, green smells of land, carried far out to
sea on off-shore winds, are appreciated long before landfall is
made. The sailors' senses had not let them down. Two days later

they caught their first sight of America, just north of Cape
Lookout, at the southern tip of the Outer Banks off the coast of
what is now North Carolina.

With a following southerly wind pushing them against a
contrary current, easing their way carefully northwards along
the edge of the low sand barriers on the seaward side of Pamlico
Sound, the English ships made slow progress for 120 miles before
they arrived at what Fernandez was looking for, a familiar gap in
the Banks he had found on earlier visits, later to be called Port
Ferdinando. With difficulty, avoiding numerous sand bars, the
ships passed through the inlet into the shallow Sound, and the
anchors crashed into the dark brown water 'about three
harquebushot within the havens mouth'. All hands were called for
a short service of thanksgiving to God for the safe arrival before
'we manned our boates, and went to view the lande next
adjoyning, and to take possession of the same, in the right of the
Queenes Majesty'.

The boat parties had landed on what is now called Bodie
Island, which, on 13 July 1584, became the first English
possession on mainland America. By the implication of Ralegh's
patent the area extended for 600 miles in every direction – so long
as it was not already possessed 'of any Christian Prynce'. The
southern limit was circumscribed by a Spanish settlement
established about twenty years earlier at Santa Elena, a mere 300
miles distant, just south of modern Charleston. This was a fact
well known to Amadas, but that would have been far from his
mind.

Bodie Island today is little like what was there in 1584. The
great Atlantic still booms on a sloping sandy beach but then the
beach was farther out to sea, and the island consequently wider.
Now the narrow banks are little more than sand hills whipped up
by strong winds into high sand dunes. In 1584 the island was
covered with pasture and forested with cedars, pines, cyprus and
oaks, offering shade to the deer and other wildlife; this has now all
disappeared through centuries of overgrazing. Modern Bodie
Island, a holiday resort, alive for the summer season and then
dead for the rest of the year, lies half a day's motoring from
Raleigh in North Carolina. Along the shore stand old, wooden,
clapboard beach cottages, like a row of grey turtles stranded
above high water mark. Not five miles from where Amadas

landed, Orville and Wilbur Wright flew the first aeroplane in 1903, when it was as remote as in Ralegh's time, for the bridge to Roanoke Island and the causeway to Bodie Island are recent, and access at the beginning of this century was by boat and ferry. Even today the place has an air of remoteness, of being at the end of the world. But for Ralegh's men it was only the beginning of the new venture.

Once landed they looked about them with wide-eyed wonder:

> wee viewed the lande about us, being whereas we first landed, very sandie, and lowe towards the water side, but so full of grapes as the very beating and surge of the Sea overflowed them, of which we founde such plentie, as well there, as in all places else, both on the sande, and on the greene soile on the hils, as in the plaines, as well as on every little shrubbe, as also climbing towardes the toppes of the high Cedars, that I thinke in all the world the like aboundance is not to be founde. . . .
>
> We passed from the Sea side towards the toppes of those hils next adjoyning, being but of meane heigth, and from thence wee behelde the Sea on both sides to the North, and to the South, finding no ende any of both waies. This lande lay stretching it selfe to the West, which wee found to be but an Island of twentie leagues long, and not above sixe miles broade. Under the banke or hill, whereon we stoode, we behelde the vallies replenished with goodly Cedar trees, and having discharged our harquebushot, such a flocke of Cranes (the most part white) arose under us, with such a crye redoubled by many Ecchoes, as if an armie of men had showted all together.

As the echoes die away all appears wonderful – the Garden of Eden rediscovered – but that was the intention of the writer, Arthur Barlow, captain of the pinnace, whose narrative of the voyage was to be used to attract investors for the main colony. After so long at sea it may have appeared as enchanting as Barlow's description, but in fact it was an inhospitable place for Europeans. Ralegh had reasoned that a Mediterranean climate would best enable a colony to become quickly self-sufficient in food. His men had landed on the 36° of latitude, admittedly the same as the Mediterranean, but on the American coast the heat of the summer is greater and the cold of winter more piercing than on any Latin shores. Citrus fruits, for example, will not grow north of 34° and mosquitoes bred in millions causing malaria and yellow fever. The Outer Banks are liable to sudden fierce storms and hurricanes born in the Caribbean, and while the beaches can look deceptively peaceful on calm days it is no place to be caught on a lee-shore when the north east wind blows shipping on to the Banks. The long chain of sandy islands gave convenient cover against the eyes of marauding Spaniards but the haven within the Banks was too shallow to allow entrance to anything bigger than a pinnace, and the constantly shifting sand bars made navigation difficult.

From the cursory examination made by Amadas and Barlow the site appeared to be completely practical and no doubt Fernandez persuaded them this was so; moreover the island was uninhabited but:

We remained by the side of this Island two whole daies, before we sawe any people of the Countrey: the third daye we espied one small boate rowing towards us. . . and we being all within boord, he walked up and downe uppon the point of the lande next unto us: then the Master, and the Pilot of the Admirall, Simon Ferdinando, and the Captaine Philip Amadas, myself [Barlow], and others, rowed to the lande, whose comming this fellowe attended, nevere making any showe of feare, or doubt. And after he had spoken of many things not understoode by us, we brought him with his owne good liking, aboord the shippes, and gave him a shirt, a hatte, and some other things, and made him taste of our wine, and our meate, which he liked very well: and after having viewed both barkes he departed and went to his owne boate againe, which hee had left in a little Cove or Creek adjoyning: assoone as hee was tow bowe shoote into the water, hee fell to fishing, and in less then halfe an howre, he had laden his boate as deepe, as it could swimme, with which he came againe to the pointe of lande, and there devided his fishe into two partes, pointing one part to the shippe, and the other to the Pinesse: which after he had (as much as he might) requited the former benefits received, he departed out of our sight.

The first encounter between the English and their Indian hosts passed off peacefully and with full politeness. The Indian was from a small tribe under their chief Wingina – whose name translated deceptively into 'Complacent-one'. Part of his tribe lived on the nearby island of Roanoke, within view of the ships, under the leadership of Wingina's brother Granganimeo (He restrains-from-ridicule) and probably numbered no more than forty-five.

They were typical of the Algonkian tribes who inhabited this part of the coastal plain. They were intelligent people but had no knowledge of iron or of the wheel, and since they had no written language, their knowledge was limited to what could be handed down in a lifetime. Their subsistence-level economy was based on fishing, hunting and the growing of three crops of maize in a summer, supplemented with beans, pumpkins and gourds. They also cultivated tobacco for smoking. Any surplus could be traded with the inland Iroquoi Indians for copper from the Great Northern Lakes, which was used for currency as well as for personal ornament. When the soil was exhausted from over-cropping, the tribe burnt out another area of forest and moved to that. The men hunted and fished and the women got on with the necessary agriculture – activities often interrupted by small local wars. This was an idyllic, finely balanced, centuries-old civilization, unable to accommodate any sudden influx of large numbers of people without severe strain. There were however political reasons why Wingina and his brother Granganimeo should welcome Amadas, Barlow and their men.

What Amadas did not know, and indeed could not know since neither he nor any of his men spoke the Indian language, was that Wingina and his tribe had recently been at war with two neighbouring tribes. Two years earlier Wingina's enemies had invited the best of his warriors and thirty women to a feast where they were treacherously killed, leaving Wingina too weak to retaliate. He and Granganimeo hoped that by treating their visitors kindly they could enlist their help in taking on their enemies.

The coastal Algonkians were already familiar with Europeans: the treacherous stormy coast, with its shoals and shallows, had seen at least two Spanish ships wrecked within living memory – memory helped by the recollection of the useful iron spikes the Indians had salvaged. And the survivors? Barlow deliberately described the Indians he saw as 'of colour yellowish, and their hair blacke for the most and yet we sawe children that had very fine aburne, and chestnut colour haire'. As for clothing, most of the Indians wore a fringed skirt of skins hanging from waist to knee; the men were distinguished by having their heads completely shaved but for a central coxcomb of hair into which was stuck a feather.

From the forest the Roanoke Indians had been carefully watching their visitors to discover if this was a casual visit of short duration or a more permanent stay. Satisfied that Amadas and his ships were not planning to leave, Granganimeo sent his friendly messenger. It must have taken considerable courage for the lone Indian to allow himself to be taken on board the strangers' ship – from a distance these people had looked peaceful, but one could never tell. The clothing offered to him made of fabric and not of the familiar skin would have been the object of wonder; similarly the food, but particularly the wine would have been a new experience – his people, strangely, had no knowledge of fermentation. Everything on board would have been so completely different from his own experience that one must pause a moment to reflect on the enterprise of this single Indian making first contact with the strange Englishmen. Used to the forest tracks and the basic life of the hutted village, he would have needed an iron nerve to carry through his mission of friendship.

To Wingina the visitors must have appeared God-sent. They had been in the Sound for three days, displayed no aggressive intent, and appeared to be self-sufficient in food. The Indians would have seen the sailors fishing – sailors will fish when there is nothing better to do – and had perhaps witnessed hunting with arquebuses, which to the Indians were miraculous and always startling when they were fired. There had been no attempt to pillage the precious stocks of Indian maize. These men would make good friends; more must be found out about them.

Who the Indians believed the Englishmen to be at this point, Barlow does not explain. Later they believed the Englishmen to be the dead returned, and so the object of respect. Early Indian religious beliefs have become so overlaid with later missionary interpretation that it is difficult to grasp what they were. Certainly the Indians held that there was a Great Spirit in the sky whose most obvious manifestation was the sun. There were lesser spirits for good and evil, and here the medicine man came into his own for only he knew the secrets for driving away the evil spirits, of which sickness was one manifestation. Unless missionary interpretation has clouded the truth, their beliefs were not altogether different from those of the English; but whereas the Indians were tolerant of the faith of others and had no missionary enthusiasm, the English were filled with bigoted confidence that Protestant Christianity was the only salvation and that the Indians were ignorant savages.

Whatever the Indian spirits told Granganimeo about his visitors, it must have been good news, for the day after his messenger's visit, Granganimeo himself paid the English a call. Barlow tells us that he arrived with forty to fifty men on the beach. His servants spread a long mat on the sand, he sitting at one end while four others of his company sat at the other. The rest of his court stood at a respectful distance. When Amadas and his company arrived on the shore, Granganimeo

> never mooved from his place, nor any of the other foure, nor never mistrusted any harme to be offered from us, but sitting still, he beckoned us to come, and sitte by him, which wee perfourmed: and beeing sette, hee makes all signes of joy, and welcome, striking on his head and breast, and afterwardes on ours, to shewe we were all one, smiling and making shewe the best hee could, of all love, and familiaritie. After hee had made a long speech unto us, wee presented him with divers thinges, which he received very joyfully, and thankefully. None of his companye durst to speake one worde all the tyme: onely the foure which were at the other ende, spake one in the others eare very softly.

Somehow it was conveyed to Amadas that Granganimeo represented his brother, the king Wingina, who was recovering from several nasty wounds (one thigh was pierced right through) suffered in a fight with a neighbouring king. Presents were exchanged, including some for Wingina; Granganimeo however made it plain that any gifts offered to his men were in fact for himself, and had them put into a basket. This first formal meeting, held on the warm sands of Bodie Island against a background of seabird cries and the swish and gurgle of the water in the sound ended, presumably, with each side satisfied of the other's friendly intent.

Within a few days both parties were trading goods: the Indians bartering skins and hides for the much valued axes and knives – weapons for the forthcoming war – and tin plates to be used for armour. The Indians tried to barter for swords, and would have given anything in exchange, but these were not for trading.

Granganimeo's curiosity was stimulated. To one whose experience went no further than canoes hollowed out of a tree trunk, the foreigners' ships must have appeared floating edifices of wonder. Barlow hints at this: 'besides they had our shippes in marvelous admiration, and all els was so strange unto them, as it appeared that none of them had ever seene the like'. But some of them may have, and while the descriptions brought back by the lone messenger were tales beyond the experience of Granganimeo, it put him at a disadvantage amongst his own men:

> After two or three daies, the Kings brother came aboord the shippes, and dranke wine, and ate of our meate, . . . and liked exceedingly thereof: and after a few daies overpassed, he brought his wife with him to the shippes, his daughter, and two or three little children: his wife was very well favored, of meane stature, and very bashfull: she had on her backe a long cloke of leather, with the furre side next to her bodie, and before her a peece of the same: about her forehead she had a broad bande of white Corrall, and so had her husband many times: in her eares she had bracelets of pearles, hanging downe to her middle . . . and those were of the bignes of good pease. The rest of her women of the better sorte, had pendants of copper, hanging in every eare, and some of the children of the Kings brother, and other Noble men, have five or sixe in every eare

In the days following bartering continued. The English tried for gold without success, and were curious about the source of the Indians' pearls. The Indians now successfully traded for the weapons they wanted.

Finally Amadas paid a visit to Granganimeo's home village on Roanoke Island. It was a long pull of around twenty miles to the north end of the island and the Englishmen's visit was seemingly unexpected for Granganimeo was absent at the time. His village consisted

> of nine houses, built of Cedar, and fortified round about with sharpe trees, to keepe out their enemies, and the entrance into it made it like a turne pike very artificially: when we came towards it, standing neere unto the waters side, the wife of Grangyno, the kings brother, came running out to meete us very cheerfully and friendly . . . some of her people she commanded to drawe our boate on the shoare, for the beating of the billoe: and others to bring our oares into the house, for feare of stealing. When we were come to the utter roome, having five rooms in her house, she caused us to sitte downe by a great fire, and after tooke off our clothes, and washed them, and dried them againe: some of the women pulled off our stockings, and washed them, some washed our feete in warme water, and shee her selfe tooke great paines to see all things ordered in the best manner shee coulde making great haste to dresse some meate for us to eate.

Granganimeo's wife rose to the occasion and, because of their importance to her husband, did her best and offered her unexpected guests considerable hospitality. Amadas and his men had been drenched either by heavy rain or water coming over the boat on the way. Granganimeo's wife sat them down by a fire in front of her hut beneath a mat awning. Here, Amadas and his men spread themselves comfortably while their clothes were washed and dried. Meanwhile, like all hostesses caught out by unexpected guests, she had done some quick thinking and by the time her visitors were dry a feast of stewed and roast venison, fish, roots, melon and other fruits was ready for them inside the hut. The feast was enjoyed until nightfall and time for sleep. Granganimeo's wife was prepared to extend her hospitality to the maximum and would have had her visitors sleep in her hut. But Amadas was taking no chances. Wisely, perhaps, he chose to sleep in the boat; it may have been that some of his men were getting too friendly with the Indian women, or he may have feared an ambush. By this time it was pouring with rain and plainly a night in the boat was going to be uncomfortable. The Indians were upset by the Englishmen's mistrust. However, their hospitality even extended to this seemingly strange whim of the visitors. Mats were lent to shelter the party and, while the boat bobbed uncomfortably off shore, thirty Indian women and some men kept watch from the beach over their snoring guests.

Amadas and his two ships remained anchored off Bodie Island for some five weeks, but Barlow is silent about what else went on during this time. It must have been spent in exploring the area and assessing its potential as well as in building up a good relationship with the Indians. Both ships had left by the end of August, Barlow returning straight to England but Amadas going on to Chesapeake Bay.[1] Amadas' visit was not welcomed by the Chesapeake Indians, and a landing party met with some hostility. Two years later one of the crew was shipwrecked on Jamaica and, when captured, told the Spaniards his version of what had taken place at Chesapeake.[2] He gave the alarming information that thirty-eight of the Englishmen had been killed and eaten by the Indians!

It is not surprising that these Indians were unwelcoming; they had suffered European molestation already. In 1570 Spanish Jesuits established a mission post on Chesapeake Bay, but they were shortly exterminated by Indians, an action savagely avenged two years later by the Spanish.[3] The Chesapeake Indians, remembering their last visitors, had every reason to attack random parties of Europeans landing in the Bay twelve years later, but they would never have eaten their enemies. From Chesapeake, Amadas tried to make for Bermuda but, blown off course in a storm, fetched up off the Azores, Fernandez' birthplace, where he remained for six weeks in a fruitless search for Spanish prizes before returning to England after a voyage lasting nine months.

Barlow, who made a more direct return to the West Country, was in England by mid-September 1584: 'we brought home also two of the Savages being lustie men, whose names were Wanchese and Manteo'. He does not add that to sail back with the Indians he had to leave two Englishmen as hostages. Wanchese (He-who-flies-out), an appropriate name in the circumstances, would eventually turn out to be a treacherous friend, but Manteo (He snatches-from-an-eagle), would prove a very good ally indeed.

With the return of Barlow and Amadas and the publicity value of Wanchese and Manteo, public interest in the venture was acute. The misadventure in Chesapeake was not mentioned and the area around Roanoke which they had explored was presented in a most favourable light, with optimism about the possibilities for exploitation. This voyage paved the way for the next in 1585.

3

'The Empty Bay'

Even before Amadas' and Barlow's return from Roanoke Island, Ralegh had begun to prepare for the next step in the programme: the despatch of colonists to form a more permanent settlement there.

In order to raise funds public interest had to be aroused, and the Queen's involvement was vital both for finance and to give investors confidence. Richard Hakluyt, propagandist for English exploration, was recruited by Ralegh to write his *Discourse of Western Planting* which was presented to the Queen on 5 October 1584. However, the Queen's response was lukewarm – or she was exercising her usual caution. At this time Amadas had returned bringing with him news of great possibilities and high expectations. The two Indians, Manteo and Wanchese became exotic objects of public wonder and quickly proved the best piece of publicity Ralegh could have devised. Further attention was brought to bear when Ralegh attempted to get a bill through Parliament confirming his rights of discovery. The Bill passed the Lords but came unstuck in the Commons and never became law. It served, however, to bring notice of the project to the influential and wealthy – the very people Ralegh needed to back him in the next stage of the venture.

In the chambers and cabinets of power Ralegh recruited his backers: Sir Richard Grenville, Ralegh's kinsman, Thomas Cavendish, shortly to be the second Englishman to sail round the world, and Anthony Rowse, a friend of Drake, all supported Ralegh's ill-fated bill and were caught up in his enthusiasm. After taking expert advice on the composition and equipment of the expedition Cavendish committed himself by contributing his own ship the *Elizabeth*, while Grenville departed to the West Country to organise shipping and finance with his friends. Meanwhile, Ralegh's dynamism was rewarded 'when he was knighted on 5 January 1585 during the course of the hectic twelve days of court celebrations of Christmas and New Year. The Queen's approval came at last: she authorised Ralegh to call his colony Virginia. More tangible was her contribution of the *Tiger* and £400 worth of gunpowder. Ralegh contributed three of his own vessels: the *Roebuck* and two pinnaces.

The Queen's *Tiger* fitted out in a Thames dockyard. She was an old ship of 160 tons' burden, originally launched in 1546 and rebuilt in 1570. Fittingly she was to lead the expedition, she being confusingly called the *Admiral*, which to Elizabethan seafarers denoted the ship as well as the rank. The remainder of the fleet was at Plymouth, and assembling it had not been uneventful. Ralegh's *Roebuck*, under Captain John Clarke, had enjoyed a full dress rehearsal for the venture by pirating in the Channel, taking the *Waterhound of Brill*. This ship was making a peaceful voyage from Nantes, with a cargo of wine and merchandise belonging to Flemish merchants, when it was set upon and captured as a prize. The fight, if there was one, was very much a one-sided affair, and soon over. She was taken into Plymouth and renamed the *Dorothy*, becoming an addition to Ralegh's fleet. The master and the pilot, both French, were not released, but carried off to the New World with the expedition, which effectively prevented them from complaining to their government.

The Channel was teeming with pirate ships of all nationalities and Clarke may have hoped that his piracy would pass unnoticed. This was not to be: the repercussions of this blatant robbery were still being felt months later, when the Dutch Ambassador wrote to Walsingham demanding that Ralegh be forced to pay the injured owners of the cargo compensation for their loss. Thanks to his influence at court Ralegh got away with that one but not with the capture by Clarke of a French prize loaded with linen and corn; the ship and cargo had to be returned. Admittedly Ralegh was given the Queen's authority to commandeer what shipping he needed in Devon, Cornwall and Bristol only, confirmation of permission being issued by licence on 10 June 1585 after the fleet had sailed.

At Plymouth the main activity above all others was the fitting out and provisioning of Ralegh's vessels. Casks of salt beef, barrels of beer, sacks of peas and flour, ship's biscuits, and crates of live squawking hens trundled through the narrow streets of the town on creaking carts. Other wagons carried barrels of gunpowder, heavy cannon, lighter falconets and calivers, with arquebuses for the soldiers who made up the fighting section of the expedition. They were heading for the main quay, where the ships were being loaded. The dockside was alive with activity. As fast as the carts were unloaded sailors in teams of three or four, swung the provisions aboard by hoists from the yard arms, their soft West Country accents mixing with the harder accents of the London seamen from the *Tiger*. High in the air went the slings on the rope hoists before plummeting down through open hatches, the bearings of the blocks or pulleys squealing above the other clamour of the dockside. Lights in the dockside taverns burnt late; all had caught Ralegh's enthusiasm for the great venture.

Somewhere in the busy life of the quays and taverns was a spy. It was not a serious matter. The Spanish Ambassador, Bernardino de Mendoza, had disgraced himself by becoming involved in the Throckmorton Plot to place Mary Queen of Scots on the English throne, and had been banished from England in 1584. He had taken up residence in Paris from where he maintained difficult contact with his spies in England. Mendoza caught wind of the expedition as early as February 1585 and sent a long report in cipher to his sovereign giving the news that a fleet of sixteen vessels was being prepared by Ralegh to take 2000 men to Norumbega, now New England. The report was so exaggerated that Walsingham's men must have been the source, feeding Mendoza the detail to frighten and mislead the Spaniards. Eventually, however, Mendoza did receive more reliable information from what must have been an eyewitness: 'At Plymouth of Rale's squadron five ships of 150 tons and eight pinnaces of about 25 tons have assembled and are preparing to sail.' By then it did not matter. The 'squadron' had sailed and was over 2000 miles away – and still Mendoza did not know whither they were bound!

Eventually the fleet was provisioned. The last water-cask had been stowed below decks; the last sacks and casks wedged tight and made fast to bulkhead bolts to prevent them coming adrift in heavy weather; and the hatches were battened down. All five ships were now ready to sail to the New World. Warped out into the harbour they lay at anchor waiting for a fair wind and tide. On 9 April 1585, Good Friday, they weighed anchor and, taking advantage of a strong north-east breeze, they passed one by one out of Plymouth harbour, the *Tiger* leading. Slowly, with little sail set, they moved out of the Cat Water between Fisher's Nose and How Stert. Setting more sail and gathering way, the line of vessels turned to port on a southerly course. As they passed St Nicholas Island they caught sight of Mount Edgecombe on the other side of the Sound. Then, with all sail set and ensigns streaming in the stiffening wind, the ships put out into the choppy Channel water. As the friendly coast of England receded astern of their fermenting wake, herring gulls screamed and swooped over scraps dropped overboard. The timbers of the small wooden ships creaked and groaned like tortured prisoners as planks worked under the movement of the sea and the invisible pressure of the wind in their sails forced the vessels onwards. Rigging hummed, halyards rattled against masts. After weeks spent in Plymouth the ships were alive again and all on board (with the exception of the two French prisoners who could only have felt apprehension) were looking forward with anticipation and excitement to the new venture.

The expedition was led by Sir Richard Grenville, styled Captain, Admiral and General, thus giving him complete authority over both military and marine personnel. Good-looking in a swashbuckling manner, he wore a bushy goatee beard and his hair was beginning to recede. In his earlier days he had sported a thinner pointed beard such as Drake favoured. Now forty-three, he was equally at home at court, at sea or with the army – a man typical of his time. He was hard-working, restless and completely involved in the matter of the moment. Born in 1542, son of Roger Grenville, Marshal of Calais, he seemed destined for a military career. His father had been drowned in 1545 when his ship, *Mary Rose*, overturned in Portsmouth Harbour. Five years later his grandfather died and the Grenville estates in Devon and Cornwall fell into the Court of Wards. The wardship of the young Richard, with the income from unsettled lands and right of marriage for the ward, were sold to a disinterested investor who shortly made over the purchase – likely enough at a profit – to Sir Hugh Paulet. Fortunately for Richard, Paulet was abroad so frequently that he had no time to dispose of the marriage advantage in the wardship and Grenville survived his years of adolescence unmarried, finally taking over his estates when he became twenty-one, in 1563. Not long afterwards he married Mary St Leger. There were two sons and four daughters of the marriage.

He fought against the Turks in Hungary in 1566, and in 1568 attempted to settle with his family in Munster, but returned to England in the following year after the Fitzmaurice rebellion, which he helped to put down. He entered Parliament in 1571 and at this time undertook a project for the discovery of *Terra Australis*, a vast continent thought to lie in the South Pacific, off South America. The scheme, approved by Elizabeth, was shortly cancelled in a fit of appeasement towards Spain who had been given rights of discovery over the western half of the globe by Pope Alexander VI in 1493. It fell to Drake to take over Grenville's plan, and, in 1580 the voyage of circumnavigation, which should have been Grenville's glorious achievement, was successfully completed by Drake who returned with unbelievable stories and more tangible treasure. Grenville's one flaw, as far as the Roanoke expedition was concerned, was that he would prove to be a bad leader of men.

Although Grenville had not been personally involved in the exploratory voyage to Roanoke in 1584 he was drawn into the bigger venture because he was Ralegh's kinsman and, when Ralegh was yet again forbidden by Elizabeth to go on so dangerous an adventure, it was natural for him to turn to this older relative, experienced in seafaring, to take his place as leader of the expedition.

With Grenville in the *Tiger* was Captain Philip Amadas. Amadas, making his second visit to Roanoke Island, was in command of the sailors on the expedition, under Grenville, while Ralph Lane, as lieutenant-general also in the *Tiger*, commanded the military arm of the venture. And with these three leaders went the boastful and temperamental Simon Fernandez, whose instability would later nearly wreck the whole project. These men, together with Cavendish, the high marshal; Francis Brooke, the treasurer; the captains of each ship; and the fourteen gentlemen who were to remain in Virginia, probably made up the general ruling council of the expedition: their number likely to prove overlarge for efficient management.

There was, too, another senior member of the party: John White. He had sailed with Amadas and Fernandez on the exploratory voyage but his earlier history is unknown. We are indebted to White for the earliest drawings of life in Virginia before it was destroyed by European settlement, for his role in the project was that of recording the natural life of the area.

The final important part of the enterprise, that of scientific recording, was to be undertaken by Thomas Hariot, working closely with John White. Hariot had been employed in Ralegh's household to instruct Ralegh in navigation and astronomy, and he had also been employed with the two Indians, Manteo and Wanchese, learning their language and as much as possible about their country.

All in all the members of the expedition offered a very wide selection of skills, and certainly one aspect of the whole was scientific investigation of a surprisingly high order. Experts had been consulted, opinions taken and, for the time, it was a venture equipped and managed by the best experience it was possible for Ralegh to hire. He had every reason to be confident of its success.

Grenville's flotilla sped down the Channel towards the Atlantic, the *Tiger* leading, followed by the *Roebuck* of 140 tons burden, the *Lion* of Chichester, 100 tons, captained by George Raymond, a part-owner, the *Elizabeth* a smaller ship of fifty tons under Thomas Cavendish, and the *Dorothy* also of fifty tons. With them went two pinnaces – small boats which might be undecked and towed astern of the *Tiger* and the *Roebuck* (or which might have been large enough to make their own course). Packed into these tiny ships were about 600 men of whom half were seamen, and the remainder soldiers, specialists and colonists.

The ships were short, squat and clumsy. For a variety of reasons it was impossible in Elizabethan times to build ships of any great size and their length was seldom more than three times that of their beam. The *Tiger* would have been about ninety feet long with a beam of about thirty: she carried 160 men. The other ships were just as uncomfortably manned. Short and square with heavy top hamper, they rolled in the slightest swell, adding to the discomfort; a nagging wife was said to be worse only than a rolling ship!

A sailor's life was pleasant only for brief intervals, the greater part of the time at sea was wretchedly uncomfortable, the food mostly inedible, the ships ill-found, leaking and pestilential. Daily rations for each man comprised an allowance of one pound of weevil-infested biscuit with one pound of salt beef or pork alternating with a quarter of a side of salt cod or ling with peas, and cheese four times a week. The thirst brought on by all the salted food was quenched by one gallon of beer per man per day. Within days of leaving port the men would be complaining of the unpleasant taste of the beer. But the flavour was not important, what mattered, but was not understood, were the bacteria multiplying by millions in the turgid depths of the beer casks as the weather became warmer. The most common infection was enteritis, a debilitating contagion which swept through crews whose natural resistance was already reduced by a totally inadequate diet. A seventeenth-century observer wrote, 'In the late Queen's time many thousands did miscarry by the corruption of drink as of meat.'[1] The wonder is that any survived at all.

Accommodation aboard was haphazard and primitive. Privacy ashore was a luxury, only for the wealthy, and it would have been naive to expect anything of the sort on board ship. Indeed, sailors had no cots or bunks until John Hawkins introduced the hammock in 1586 after seeing West Indians taking siestas in the contraptions. On board the *Tiger* and the rest of the small fleet, the men would have slept where they could and were lucky if the deck was cushioned by a friendly coil of wet rope. Social life ashore was reflected aboard. The Admiral, Generals and Captains, as being the most senior ranks, dined in the great cabin, the equivalent of the Great Chamber ashore. The officers, being gentlemen, and the gentlemen passengers dined in their own mess, but in rather less style. The rest of the company had their own messes, no doubt reflecting their rank in the hierarchy as in the great halls of the larger households ashore.

The food was prepared in the cook-room, usually placed well down in the ship, the only place on board with a hearth, though a fire was only possible in comparatively calm weather. But while the crew might have their meals served hot from a pail, in the great cabin life was more civilized. Gold and silver plate was set out for the wealthy and wine took the place of the seaman's beer. Musicians played and food was served with the same colourful pageantry which men of this rank expected at home.

On the second day out, the fleet was overtaken by a violent storm in the Bay of Biscay; it endured through Easter Day.

Fernandez should have been forewarned of this by the 'Prognostications' of William Bourne in his almanack for 1585, which he undoubtedly would have carried aboard with his other books on navigation: 'This season of the yeare is likely windy and cloudy. Towards the end of April such winde . . .' And the wind which blew so fiercely scattered the fleet and sank the *Tiger's* pinnace – or else they cast it off. Flying on the black wings of night, Grenville arrived alone off the Canaries five days after leaving Plymouth. At fourteen knots average running before the storm this must have been a record for the time.

The Canaries were no place to linger; for reports of the ship's arrival would have been carried straight to King Philip of Spain in his vast and remote palace of the Escorial. Setting a west-south-west course for Dominica in the Caribbean, the pre-arranged rendezvous with the other four vessels, Grenville followed the customary southerly route which was to become so familiar to many members of the company.

The *Tiger* sped into the Atlantic on fresh north-easterly trade winds. Flying fish, frightened by the vessel's passage, darted out of the water, skimming the tops of waves, while the gulls deserted them as they sailed further and further from land. The warm, clean, balmy breezes of the Canaries would turn hotter on the gradual passage southwards. The friendly, following sea lifted the stern high, suddenly to drop it again in hurried forward surges, carrying them on towards exciting and unknown adventures.

The *Tiger's* log for the voyage is lost, and there are only bare extracts from a journal probably written up later by Barlow, which makes no mention of the Biscay storm. The Atlantic crossing is covered by a mere dozen words. This may have been one of those brief, pleasant intervals in a sailor's hard life. Provided the wind remained steady, sails could be set and left aloft, with no need for tedious tacking: the trade winds were taking them straight to their rendezvous. The bosun's whistle calling the watch to trim the yards to catch every pressure of wind, was the only necessary attention to sailing. The look-out on the foremast was ever watchful for a distant sail either friendly or, with luck, Spanish to attack and take as a prize. To supplement the unhealthy salt diet, it was possible, too, to catch fish from a trailing line. Torn sails could be mended now, and clothes washed by towing them astern on a line – if the sailors bothered at all. One of the seamen, taking advantage of the warm tropical water, was washing himself over the side of the ship when he had a leg bitten off by a shark. Men had time to sit on deck on warm nights under the full or waning moon, talking of experiences past and adventures to come. These may have been halcyon days.

During the long Atlantic crossing the assorted personalities aboard the *Tiger* also had time to discover each other's weaknesses. On an earlier voyage, Fernandez, boasting of his skill as a horseman 'which is a thing few mariners can well doe', left his observer wondering whether his navigation was worse than his horsemanship for, as was commented dryly, Fernandez had by his own calculation 'sayled a month on dry land'.[2] The pilot was an uncomfortable man to sail with, and had made enemies on previous voyages. This one would be no exception. Grenville, himself, was not beyond criticism, and was said to act in an imperious and arbitrary fashion. He was certainly hostile to Fernandez, with whom Lane sided against Grenville. Enmities and factions are easily formed in small cramped quarters where every move and nuance is noted and none escapes. The ill-matched temperaments in the great cabin of the *Tiger* generated a dangerous atmosphere which smouldered throughout the expedition.

The *Tiger* maintained its speed and just four weeks and 3000 miles after leaving the Canaries astern, landfall was made at Dominica on 7 May 1585. In this instance Fernandez' navigation was faultless, as no doubt he announced to all, but with a following wind and no need to calculate traverses, his problems had been minimal. John White took this opportunity to draw an outline view of Dominica as a guide to future voyagers. Turning on a north-westerly course, after three days the look-out sighted St Croix Island off their starboard bow, then, passing down the southern coast of Puerto Rico, Grenville landed his men on the small uninhabited island of Cotesa, just to the south-east of Guayanilla Point, to refresh and recharge the company which had been so long cooped up on board. (The southern coast of Puerto Rico was the least inhabited part of the island; San Juan, the capital, was on the northern side.)

But if Grenville thought he was unobserved he was mistaken. Their arrival was immediately reported to the Governor, Diego

Menéndez de Valdés, who posted forty men to watch the English. Staying no more than a day at Cotesa, Grenville next moved on to the safer anchorage of Mosquetal – now called Tallaboa – Bay, on another small island, St John, which was the prearranged rendezvous for the other members of the scattered fleet. Rounding the headland into Mosquetal Bay on 12 May and moving slowly through the clear tropical water the *Tiger* 'came to anker ... within a Fawlcon shot of the shoare'.

There was no sign of any of the other four vessels. The Bay was empty!

4

'The Manner of the Seas'

To Sir Richard Grenville the emptiness of Mosquetal Bay gave little cause for concern; he had made a fast crossing and could afford to wait for the arrival of the smaller ships. And there was plenty to do to fill in the time. The crew were ready to stretch their legs, water casks had to be refilled, fresh food taken aboard, and above all there was time to build a pinnace to replace that lost in the storm. (A pinnace was essential for exploring the shallow inland waters of the Outer Banks in Virginia.)

Remaining at anchor 'a Fawlcon shot' from the shore, the *Tiger* was left manned by forty sailors – one watch – while the rest – 120 in all – went ashore to build a fort on the beach. This was protected on one side by a freshwater river, drawing from a marshy inland plain, and on the other by a shallow lake. John White made a very detailed drawing of the Mosquetal fort (see illustration). If his scale is accurate then it measured 600 feet by 500 feet, a more than adequate enclosure to protect the camp. The form of the fort, however, would have been dictated by the position of the lake and the river and this may account for its having been larger than was needed. From the river to the lake, and from there to the beach, an outer defensive ditch was dug, backed on the inside by a bank of earth. The ditch then extended along the beach, but here the defences were reversed, with the ditch inside and the bank outside the camp. The purpose of this latter defence was not to protect the camp inside the fort but, in the event of a forced evacuation of the fort, to provide cover for a rearguard defending the shore while the main party was ferried out to the *Tiger*. It was always intended that Mosquetal fort should be defended from seaward by the *Tiger*: it was not to be an independent strong point for a land-based force.

White's drawing shows the new pinnace being built inside the fort, close to the beach. On the east (the right-hand side) is a forge, for making nails for the new boat, and beyond the enclosure, outside the defences twelve men are straining at the ropes of a four-wheeled cart carrying a tree trunk, brought from as much as four miles away for the building of the pinnace. It is difficult to know why, when the pinnace is so nearly finished, there should be any need for the huge piece of timber being dragged with so much toil towards the fort. Behind the cart and guarding it are twenty-six soldiers. Just inside the north parapet before a large hut, is marked 'Mr Lanes quarter' and to the south, along the seaward side, are five round huts marked 'The Generalls quarter', defended by four guards. General Sir Richard Grenville is seen returning to camp on horseback from the far bank of the river to a welcoming salute from two sentinels firing off harquebuses. Offshore, in a blue sea, the *Tiger* rides at anchor.

The original attraction of St John's Island as a rendezvous for the fleet had been its remoteness. Someone on the *Tiger* must have been there before. Fernandez and, by inference, John White and Barlow had all been on the 1584 exploration, and although Barlow's official account of that voyage makes no mention of stopping at St John's, fresh water must have been taken aboard in the West Indies and St John's is the likely harbour. In spite of the isolation of St John's, the Spaniards were watching and reporting everything to their base on the island, St German, which had been established after Barlow's voyage and therefore was unknown to Grenville. When the Spanish commander at Puerto Rico received these reports he was understandably alarmed. The small force of 120 men had become 400; the fort 'A great breastwork . . . with a moat, and a long stretch of beach enclosed with trenches, huts erected and a smithy; and all in as great perfection as though they had proposed to remain there ten years'.[1] From this report the Governor had every reason to think that the islands were about to be invaded and permanently occupied. Exaggerated as the details undoubtedly were, they were in one respect true; the fort may have been planned as a semi-permanent base for supply ships on course for Virginia for they would need to take in fresh water and supplies en route and what better place than a remote island off Puerto Rico?

After some days lurking unseen in the woods the Spaniards revealed themselves. 'The 16 Day [May], there appeared unto us out of the woods 8 horsemen of the Spaniards, about a quarter of a myle from our Porte, staying about halfe an hower in viewing our forces: but as soone as they saw $\overline{X}$ of our shot marching towards them, they presently retyred into the woodes.' Outnumbered, the Spaniards remained discreetly observing and completely puzzled as to English intentions.

On 19 May 1585, the eighth day of occupation, a distant sail was sighted by the look-out. As it came over the horizon the *Tiger*, reinforced by some of the shore party, weighed anchor and went out with all guns cleared to challenge the intruder. This was a worrying moment for Grenville who, not knowing how many armed Spaniards surrounded him, had to divide his force between the fort and the ship, leaving each with a reduced complement. The approaching sail, at first showing only a topsail above the shimmering horizon, was watched as keenly by the Spaniards as by the English from their lower exposed position on the beach. Slowly the unknown sail crawled over the edge of the world.

The crew of the *Tiger* recognised the good news first. The strange sail was the *Elizabeth*, the smallest of the fleet, commanded by Thomas Cavendish, coming up to keep the rendezvous at St John's. To signal the good news to those ashore, the *Tiger* fired off a salute 'according to the manner of the Seas'. The sudden explosion of gunfire echoing across the water seemed, to those in the fort, like the opening of a sea-battle, but when there followed an answering broadside from the stranger, they understood the signal. A cheer must have gone up and tension relaxed as the two ships came to anchor in the bay. Grenville now had over 200 men and his relief must have known no bounds.

With this happy change of circumstances new plans had to be made. The crew of the *Elizabeth* needed to refresh themselves, to take on water. And, of course, there was still a chance that the other three vessels from the scattered fleet would arrive. As the pinnace was still under construction it was apparent that a few more days at St John's were needed. If the Spaniards had intended to attack they would have done so when Grenville's forces were at their weakest. Clearly there was everything to be gained by spending a few more days at St John's Island.

Two days after the *Elizabeth*'s arrival, twenty Spanish

horsemen appeared on the other side of the river. With some concern Grenville sent a party of twenty footsoldiers with two men mounted on horses taken earlier from the Spanish to meet them. This was not an aggressive gesture by the Spaniards. As the English approached the mounted party they were obviously at a disadvantage but the Spanish leader, by signs, asked for a parley and showed his sincerity with a flag of truce. The two groups faced each other across the hot sand, while two men from each side met on the middle line of the neutral ground.

The Spaniards began by proudly denouncing the English for appropriating and fortifying the Spanish beach; to which the two English replied that their intention was not war but simply to re-victual their ships and, as for other necessities, rather than take what they needed by force they were prepared to barter and trade. The meeting ended when the Spanish agreed to meet Grenville the following day to trade for the necessary supplies. White's drawing shows Grenville returning on horseback immediately after the meeting with the Spaniards, although the account does not say that he went to the parley. The shadows show it is late afternoon, and the pinnace is all but finished, ready to be launched the following day. Two of the captured Spanish horses run amongst the trees in the middle of the fort, and although the anonymous account tells us that the two horsemen went to parley with the Spanish only one is shown returning. Furthermore one would have thought that with the Spaniards on the other bank all hands would have been at armed standby. It is likely that the drawing shows several separate events in time, in the manner of a medieval drawing.

The next day, after the successful launching of the new pinnace, Grenville marched up country with his captains and gentlemen to the agreed meeting place. But the Spaniards had arranged the parley in order to examine the fort more closely and to assess the strength of the English force. Inevitably Grenville waited in vain for the Spanish 'who keeping to their old custome for perjurie and breache of promise came not'. In revenge Grenville rather pointlessly set fire to the woods before returning to the fort. Once returned, and immediately suspicious of the treacherous Spaniards, Grenville ordered all men and equipment on board the two vessels to be ready to sail at dawn. The fort had become too interesting to the Spaniards to be

comfortable for Grenville, too uncomfortable too for his men
ashore, bothered in the increasing heat by fearsome mosquitoes
which could pierce even very thick clothing. Grenville had no
desire to become involved in land fighting to no advantage; the
fort would have to be adandoned. For any of the missing three
vessels which might arrive later, a message in gothic lettering was
carved into a tree trunk: 'On May 11th we reached this place
with the *Tiger* and on the 19th the *Elizabeth* came up and we are
about to leave on 23rd, Glory be to God 1585.'[2]

As the two ships rocked at anchor in the bay that night the
watch paced the deck turning the time glass every half-hour and
striking the ship's bell to mark the passing time. In the great
cabin of the *Tiger*, laterns burnt late as the council, consisting of
Grenville, Cavendish, Fernandez, Lane, White and Hariot
discussed the best course to set for Spanish prizes. What the
Spaniards would not barter for would have to be taken in other
ways; items such as horses, pigs and poultry were essential for the
colony's survival. Over the noise of the general discussion the
sound of the ship's bell drifted through from the main deck.
Ashore and unseen, the Spanish watchers lay in the dark,
waiting. Above the hubbub of the jungle night-life the ships' bells
could be heard across the water as well as West Country voices
occasionally shouting from ship to ship . The Spaniards had
noted the loading of the two vessels and had seen all those ashore
return aboard. Waiting for the coming dawn they watched and
speculated.

5

'Trumpets and Consort of Music'

As soon as light came the following day, the two ships and the newly launched pinnace were noisy with activity. The shrill sound of the bosun's whistle, preceding a shouted order, pierced the warm morning air, and the wooden deck rumbled under the thud of the seamen's bare feet as they scurried aloft to set sail on the dew-soaked yards and sheets. Slowly the vessels put out of the bay and, gathering way in the open sea, set an easterly course for the channel lying between Puerto Rico and Hispaniola.

Ashore the Spaniards watched their unwelcome guests leave and came out of the shelter of the trees to examine the deserted fort. No doubt the English vessels were by then still near enough to shout some obsenity to the foreigners in the still, clear air. Later the Spaniards reported that they found nothing except the unfathomable message carved into the tree trunk. In the mounting heat of the early summer day they struggled, perspiring, to uproot the unwilling stump – it was more unyielding than they first imagined, for the Englishmen never intended it to be removed. By the time the armed party returned through the jungle to their base, in the north of the island, cursing under the effort of transporting the damnable stump, Grenville and his two escorting vessels were patrolling the Mona Channel off Puerto Rico, lying in wait for rich Spanish prizes. On land a small reinforcement of thirty-five harquebusiers, sent to help the Spanish lieutenant and his forty men, were recalled when it was clear that the English ships were leaving and St John's was, for the moment at least, free from the danger of invasion. But the Spaniards were not free of their worry about the carved message. Once it had arrived at St German there was the problem of finding someone to translate it: 'wretched writing' was one comment. Painfully deciphered and its meaning reported to a higher authority at Havana the message told them nothing they did not know already. The English had left St John's.

The *Tiger* and the *Elizabeth* on the look-out for prizes, did not have long to wait. On the evening of the day they left Mosquetal Bay, they came upon a bark in the Mona Channel making its way from Santo Domingo to Puerto Rico. If either the *Tiger* or the *Elizabeth* had time to clear their guns for action it was unnecessary; the crew of the bark took to their boat and disappeared overside rowing hard for the distant shoreline before a warning shot was fired. The bark, either French or Spanish, was taken with no trouble but was empty of cargo. A prize crew was put on board to sail the captured vessel.

Better luck followed. Early next morning, in the light of the almost full moon, a large frigate was sighted making a course from Santo Domingo to Puerto Rico. Unlike the earlier prize, she carried a valuable cargo of cloth transhipped from the *flota* recently arrived from Spain with supplies for the islands. Before the sun rose this ship too gave up without a fight. Not only was there a valuable cargo aboard but passengers too – 'divers Spaniards of accompt'.

The cargo and prisoners were of little practical use to the settlers but Grenville now had a bargaining counter to force the Spaniards to part with the supplies needed for his colony. The two prizes had given themselves up peacefully, as if they knew their part in the deal. The passengers were transferred to the *Tiger* and another prize crew put on board the captured vessel. Grenville's ships were now becoming undermanned and it was time to call a halt to further captures. The four vessels, with the new pinnace which had been invaluable for boarding the prizes, turned into a nearby anchorage to await the reply to a message sent to St German that Grenville wished to trade. The wish to trade with the enemy was not as outrageous as it appears. It had become the practice in the islands for the French merchants based there to trade with the English and French privateers for the goods plundered on the Spanish trade routes. The captured booty was then sold back to the Spanish through the French merchants. This had a practical advantage for the Spanish; they got their cargoes back relatively quickly and without the full expense of replacing the missing goods and the cost of the long voyage from Spain. No doubt the corsairs took these costs into account and were reasonable in their prices. The practice was firmly banned by the Escorial Palace in far away Spain but communication was slow and the custom had a great deal to recommend it to those living in the Caribbean. In Grenville's case a strange interlude followed for which he was fully prepared and which he may even have expected.

The pilot, Fernandez, was familiar with the islands and had visited those parts many times before. He also had a friend, Alanson, living on Hispaniola. Alanson was probably one of the French merchants who dealt in the illegal business of trading for captured cargoes, and it was through Alanson that Grenville and Fernandez established a line of communication with the Spaniards, and with him they were making secret arrangements to trade. So secret were these arrangements that few of the other members of Grenville's council were aware of what was going on.

Ralph Lane was one kept ignorant of what Grenville was up to. He was deputed to take the smaller of the two captured vessels to find salt. This essential commodity for survival, as important then as it is today, was one supply which Grenville could obtain without trading. With Lane went twenty-six men, including soldiers to guard the six Spanish prisoners with them, one being a Spanish pilot who was to guide them. Armed with spades and mattocks as well as conventional weapons, Lane sailed off unwillingly. He was nervous about the whole proposition, believing that he had insufficient men to fight off the superior Spanish detachments he was certain he would meet. The pilot guided the vessel to Rojo Bay on the south-west side of St John's, and there on the beach were two salt mounds – the result of someone else's efforts – ready for the taking. Immediately on landing, Lane threw up a rough bank and ditch to enclose both heaps and posted a look-out on top of the highest (see illustration). The prisoners set to with spades and mattocks, loading the salt into casks and rowing the heavy loads over to the bark anchored just off shore. For three days the backbreaking and gruelling work went on. Once, to confirm Lane's worst apprehensions, they were watched by a party of Spanish horsemen and troops. At this moment of Lane's ordeal surprisingly, no attack was made. The Spaniards moved off, apparently satisfied with what they observed. At last the final cask was loaded and, with certain relief, Lane abandoned his beach-head and returned to Grenville with the precious salt.

Once back in the protective security of the fleet, Lane released the tension of the last three days by making his views strongly known to Grenville. As if his tribulations on the beach, mainly imagined, had not been enough, he was particularly enraged to find that while he had been on what he saw as a dangerous mission, Grenville had been trading with the Spaniards in the vicinity of Guayanilla, and one of the prizes had been offered for sale. Grenville had also attempted to ransom the prisoners but whether ransomed or not they had been released. He had acquired, too, pigs, cattle and horses. Lane considered that his small party had been dangerously employed to lure the garrison away whilst Grenville used the interlude for successful barter, without taking Lane into his confidence. It was this last point which rankled most: something had been going on behind Lane's back. He had every reason for resentment. The Spaniards at Rojo Bay could easily have attacked his small party when they were exhausted by the heavy work; his prisoners would have turned on him, and all would have been lost. Yet the Spaniards, fully aware that Lane was there, had left the party alone. Clearly they knew of the main trading arrangement with Grenville and Lane did not. We should not suspect malice on Grenville's part, however. He was simply not a good leader, which showed in his failure to communicate.

On 1 June 1585 the small but impressive fleet sailed round to Isabela on the north side of Hispaniola. The prisoners, whom Grenville had let fly in the manner of doves of peace, had preceded him and, as he had intended, had told the Alcalde an eloquent tale of a great English lord called 'Verde Campo' (a near Spanish translation of Grenville for Green Field) who had come to settle the remote parts of Dominica and Trinidad, unused by the Spaniards. They wished to settle in peace, reported the released hostages, and to trade with the Spanish colonists. The expedition was impressively described: it included men of all trades as well as twenty gentlemen; the two tall Indians were curiously noted; food was served on gold and silver plate; and the English had brought with them musical instruments such as clarions and organs, and a Protestant bible translated into Spanish. John White was even reported drawing banana plants and fruit trees, and it was noted that Grenville had already tried, unsuccessfully, to trade for horses and cattle on St John's Island. The Alcalde was impressed, so impressed he sent a message to Grenville that he would pay him a visit in a day or so.

Accordingly, two days later, Captain Rengifo de Angulo, the Alcalde of Isabela and the warden of the fort, accompanied by a 'lusty friar' and twenty gentlemen and attended by their servants and negro slaves, arrived on the foreshore opposite Grenville's ships.[1]

In their vividly coloured clothes, against a background of waving palms, they made an exotic and splendid spectacle. Grenville immediately lowered his boats and headed for the shore with an even bigger reception party. So large was Grenville's escort that the Spaniards at first refused to let all of the boats land. But the warm friendliness between Grenville and Angulo, the gentlemen and the lesser ranks from both sides, convinced the Spaniards that they had nothing to fear, and the rest of Grenville's party was allowed onto the beach.

There followed one of the strangest impromptu picnics of all time. While Grenville and Angulo, beneath the shade of the trees on the beach, talked of the island, its products and population, the English party put up two banqueting houses or shelters covered with palm fronds to keep off the heat of the mid-day sun – one cover for the gentlemen, of course, and the other for the rest of the party. To the sound of 'trumpets and consort of musick' a vast and sumptuous banquet was served on the edge of the tropical beach. It was an incident of splendour. No doubt the high table was laid with beautiful carpet cloths and set with gold plate. Dish after dish of gold and silver plate filled with impressive fare (or as impressive as the temporary circumstance permitted) was carried to the tables. It is not explained how the menus were prepared, nor what was offered, but the occasion was splendid propaganda, fully appreciated by the Spaniards. Eventually, the banquet accomplished, the Spaniards sent off to the mountains for three white bulls and provided a saddled horse for every gentlemen who wished to join in the bullfight which followed. The bulls were goaded for three hours on the hot beach until at last all were put out of their frightened agony. One was killed by a musket ball and another took to the sea in fearful desperation before it met its end. The honours of that strange day were concluded by exchanges of extravagant presents.

The Spaniards were now convinced of Grenville's sincerity and the next day was given over to the purpose of the whole pageant: trading. It is not revealed if the captured cloth was bartered but it almost certainly was; the Spaniards had greater need of it anyway. By the end of the day, the English had added not only more horses, cattle and pigs to their livestock but now had bulls for breeding, goats and root plants – all for the sustenance and establishment of the settlers. Grenville also traded for hides, pearls, ginger and tobacco for sale on his return to England. He was capitalising on his booty. With this crucial business accomplished, on 7 June the English fleet sailed from Hispaniola on a north-westerly course, both sides congratulating themselves on their astuteness. While no official report of this impressive fraternising has been found in Spanish archives – for to have mentioned anything would have brought down royal wrath to no one's advantage – the English threat had been bought off without damage.

It happened that Pedro Menéndez Marqués, the nephew of the Spaniard responsible for the savage revenge taken on the Chesapeake Indians for the annihilation of the Jesuit mission in 1572, had been granted leave to return to Spain from Florida and had arrived at Havana when he heard that Grenville was off Puerto Rico. In 1577 Menéndez Marqués had been sent with reinforcements to the Spanish settlements on mainland America.[2] His mission was to expel or exterminate any foreign settlements – namely the French who were the only other intruders in America at the time – and to stamp out any Indian opposition. This he had done successfully and, since 1581, had been trying to get leave to return home. The rumours of Gilbert's expedition in 1580, however, followed by Ralegh's plans of founding a settlement, had been passed on to Spain by Mendoza, furtively spying from Paris. These alarming reports had prevented Marqués' recall, and it was his bad luck that Grenville should arrive in the Carribbean when he was on his way home. That the expedition included two Indians caused Menéndez Marqués to fear that Grenville intended landing his colony in the Spanish orbit of Florida (the area of Florida was understood by the Spanish to run a great deal further north than it now does).

The unfortunate man again deferred his journey to Spain and regretfully returned to his base at San Agustín in Florida to spend the autumn building a new fort and searching for Grenville. He was a conscientious man, isolated on the edge of a huge and unknown continent. Sighing for his familiar and distant homeland he wanted to end his exile quickly – but also to conclude his mission successfully.

Approaching the mainland of America, ahead of Menéndez Marqués, and loaded with noisy, mooing, snorting and neighing livestock, resembling a small fleet of Noah's arks, was Grenville in the *Tiger* escorted by the *Elizabeth*, the newly built pinnace, sailing awkwardly, and the two prizes. They made a short stop at an island for seal hunting, where Grenville nearly wrecked the pinnace. Another stop was made at an island wrongly identified by Fernandez as a source of salt. And two more short stops were made before the coast of Florida was sighted on 20 June 1585. Slowly Fernandez probed his way along the coastline on a north-easterly course, looking for familiar landmarks. In rounding Cape Lookout disaster was only just averted, when the *Tiger* was all but driven ashore in a combination of shoal water and tide rips. The following day, 24 June, and seventeen days since leaving Hispaniola, they anchored in the shelter of the Outer Banks. Here the main party of settlers went ashore to make their first landing on American soil. The anonymous writer of the *Tiger* journal reports a great catch of fish at this time. After a brief stop the English were on their way again, holding the same north-easterly course; Fernandez had at last got his bearings.

The long voyage across the Atlantic in small ships had produced the usual frictions between leaders and men of lesser rank. Lane had his knife into Grenville, particularly since the episode of Rojo Bay. He had also fallen out with the treasurer, Francis Brook, and others. The writer of the *Tiger* journal (perhaps Arthur Barlow) was very critical of Fernandez and his ability. Two factions had thus formed up – one behind Grenville and against Fernandez, the other supporting Fernandez and Walsingham's men. This disunity, fomented on the long voyage, would later come to a head.

Two days after the reported catch of fish Fernandez safely brought his fleet to Wococon Island where they anchored offshore. Now they were in an area familiar to all those who had sailed in 1584 with Barlow. As this was a dangerous and treacherous coast, with shifting sand and sudden storm, a few days may have been spent in sounding out the entrance channel. It is not clear why Fernandez should have attempted an entrance to Pamlico Sound through such a hazardous passage, for the familiar Port Ferdinando was only eighty miles to the north. But Wococon may have been a prearranged rendezvous for the scattered fleet; it was well out of sight of Wingina's people on Roanoke Island. Nevertheless it would have been naive to expect that a prolonged wait would have gone unreported to Wingina. If his own men had not seen the ships, the news would have come from his neighbours.

In any event the soundings were to no avail, for the *Elizabeth* and the two prizes ran on to sand bars in the channel but were refloated without damage. Not so the *Tiger*. She too struck a sand bar and was held fast for two terrifying hours whilst heavy rollers threatened to break up the ship. Keeled over with her cargo shifted – making the job of salvage doubly difficult – the *Tiger* was at last freed – but only at a price. Her timbers had been severely strained, she was leaking and had taken a great deal of water below. Her condition was so serious that it was impossible to sail her and she was run hard onto the beach. Serious also was the condition of the supplies below deck: the corn, malt, meat, rice and other provisions had all been saturated by sea water and completely ruined. In those two long hours the future of the unborn colony hung in the balance. Happily no lives had been lost and, as the *Tiger's* keel was not fractured, she was repairable, but it was a salutary lesson on the dangers of the coast. The writer of the *Tiger's* journal, one of Grenville's supporters, laid the entire blame for the mishap on Fernandez.

Battered and shaken, with a great part of their provisions lost, the colonists had now all but arrived at their destination. In one respect they could congratulate themselves that no life had been lost through accident, disease or enemy action in the adventurous six weeks since they left Plymouth Sound: Lane attributed this to a 'discipline' he had devised. In another respect – in addition to the near loss of the *Tiger* and the complete loss of the greater part of their stores – there was cause for concern. In Pamlico Sound, and off the coast which shimmered and undulated in the summer heat, there were no other vessels. The *Tiger* and the *Elizabeth* with their acquired escorts, were alone; of the *Lion*, the *Dorothy*, the *Roebuck*, and the small flyboat, there was still no sight nor sign. It must have been very much in Grenville's mind that it might not be possible to establish a settlement on this expedition after all.

6

'Towne of Pomeiock'

Here we must take up the story, as far as it can be told, of what had become of the missing vessels – the *Lion*, the *Dorothy*, the *Roebuck*, and the surviving pinnace – of Grenville's fleet after the storm in the Bay of Biscay had scattered the ships. The tale of the *Lion*, the second largest after the *Tiger*, reveals the hazards endured by Elizabethan seafarers.

The *Lion*, accompanied by the pinnace, crossed the Atlantic and arrived in the Caribbean. Missing the usual route to Florida by way of the Mona Channel, the *Lion* was on a northerly course and rounding Point Negril at the west end of Jamaica when she came on a Frenchman.[1] A sea fight followed, which the English claimed to have won; since the Frenchman got away the result is open to question. After this inconclusive fight, witnessed by some Jamaicans from the safety of the shore, three Englishmen landed on Point Negril. Whether their arrival was by accident or design is not explained; they may have fallen overboard in the fight or have been shipped ashore as a punishment for wrongdoing. One shortly died and the other two were captured. One of the prisoners was taken to the Marqués of Villalobos, abbot of Jamaica, and his official note of the interrogation which followed has a ring of truth.

The Marqués was attempting to find out if the man knew what the *Lion* was doing in the area. The prisoner, he reported, 'spoke thickly and knew no Latin'; he was, no doubt, a West Countryman. He obstinately refused to answer questions about his religion and beliefs – leading questions in any Spanish enquiry. Finally the poor man, fearing the worst and goaded to proud despair, blurted out; 'So much commending to God! Hang me and have done with it!' Whatever information the devout but bigoted Abbot may have gleaned about the intentions of the *Lion* was only part of the story: he had to wait until June the following year to hear more.

In the mid-summer of 1586 a castaway from the *Lion* was found wandering in Jamaica and taken, as a matter of course, to the Marqués. The prisoner's name was Edwards, a gentleman and an accountant sailing under 'Don Ricardus gran field' (another attempt by the Spanish at the difficult name of Grenville). Unfortunately the Marqués understood no English and Edwards spoke no Spanish, and between the two their misunderstandings left much ambiguous detail, but the main story of the *Lion*'s voyage can be pieced together.

The *Lion* arrived off Jamaica in some distress and with most of her provisions used. George Raymond, her captain, took one of those decisions which Elizabethans had no trouble in taking: to preserve dwindling stores he abandoned the useless members of the ship's company, in this case the soldiers. All twenty of them were dumped, protesting, on Spanish Jamaica to perish or survive as best they could. It is ironic that Raymond could easily have provided his crew with provisions from the forests of Jamaica, but preferred to continue the voyage supported by the unhealthy and unappetising salt meat and fish taken on board in England. The soldiers had no sooner got their bearings than they made a stupid decision. They split into two groups, and one party of nine men, including their captain, John Copletope, disappeared into the interior of Jamaica, never to be heard of again. Edwards wisely stayed on the coast with the remaining party of eleven. In retrospect it seems quite astonishing that, on a lush and fruitful island surrounded by seas teeming with fish, Edwards claimed that nine of the party died of hunger; he said that he watched their wretched end.

If these unfortunate men were unable to survive on Jamaica it is just as well they never reached Virginia for they would only have been a liability. Of the two survivors Edwards, who told the tale, was shipped off to Spain to be cross-examined by King Philip when the Marqués had finished with him. He too was never heard of again.

With fewer crew, the *Lion* made good time to the rendezvous, arriving off Croatoan Island on 17 June 1585, four days before the *Tiger* even sighted the coast of America. Croatoan Island lay some fifty miles south of Roanoke, but only fifteen miles north of the Wococon passage where the *Tiger* went aground. Here on Croatoan, Raymond landed thirty colonists and met up with the *Dorothy*.

High and dry on the beach at Wococon, with all stores and movables taken off her, the *Tiger* was careened over by a line made fast to her main-mast until one side of her hull was clear enough of the beach for work to begin fixing the strained planks which had worked loose in the awful pounding she had taken on the sand bar on 29 June. The gaps between her sprung timbers were caulked with tow and pitch, and with one half of her hull repaired and made watertight, the *Tiger* was then careened onto her other side. The work was completed in the third week of July and, taking advantage of the high spring tides of that month, the vessel was warped off the beach by anchors laid off shore. Once the *Tiger* was safely afloat again, her stores, such as had been unspoilt, were reloaded. It is likely that the opportunity was taken to bream some of the other vessels at this time, by careening them and burning off the growth of weed below the waterline, which collected all too quickly in tropical waters and took knots off the speed.

Meanwhile, on 3 July 1585, Grenville sent word of his arrival to Wingina on Roanoke Island and from Wingina he learnt that the *Lion* and the *Dorothy* had arrived off the Outer Banks. News of their safe landfall had come to Grenville, however, even before the Roanoke party returned. Two of Grenville's captains were sent north to explore the area of Croatoan, where they met up with two of the thirty colonists set down by the *Lion* three weeks earlier. It did not take long to round up the remaining twenty-eight. After dropping the party of colonists, the *Lion* had not stopped. Accompanied by her pinnace, like a shark with its pilot fish, she had continued on a northerly course for Newfoundland. This was part of a pre-arranged and complicated plan which will be discussed later.

Some time in the second week of July, Grenville made contact with the *Dorothy* and the *Roebuck*. Having accounted for all his fleet, Grenville himself now began exploring the area, making sensible use of the time to explore the southern end of Pamlico Sound while the repairs to the *Tiger* continued. Taking the new pinnace, a four-oared wherry, and two other boats, Grenville set off with five of his captains, Hariot and John White, and sixty men. Almost immediately they ran into trouble. The pinnace proved too cumbersome to be rowed and its draught too deep to clear the many shallow sand-bars in this lower end of the Sound: the boat was quite unfit for the purpose for which it had been designed. This left only three boats to take them through the shallows. The wherry, carrying fifteen men, their baggage and provisions, was a substantial weight to pull through the water. Grenville, his captains and gentlemen, did not travel light on these sorties, taking with them their armour or breastplates (which were heavy pieces of equipment) as well as a multitude of firearms, sidearms and swords. This time they also took silver cups and plates for impressive ceremonial occasions, and no doubt trumpets for sounding orders and musical instruments to accompany dining. One boat was equipped with an awning, a luxury reserved for Grenville and his gentlemen. The sailors were left to their grilling work under the full heat of the July sun, although the waters of the Sound would at least have been cooled by the merciful sea breeze.

Grenville's first stop was at the Indian village of Pomeiooc, which lay at the mouth of a small inlet now known as Gibbs Creek. This was Grenville's first encounter with Indian civilisation and it was also the subject of John White's first drawing of America (see illustration) White shows us eighteen huts enclosed by a palisade of vertical stakes. The huts are built of mats hung on a wooden frame, the largest hut belonging to the chief, or werowance; inside can be seen his sleeping benches. Indians stand about, one busy splitting wood with an axe – perhaps obtained from trading with Barlow the year before – another with a fox-like dog. (This is the earliest illustration of an American domestic dog.) In the clear centre of the village burns a fire, around which a group of Indians, sitting and kneeling on mats, are engaged in a ceremony involving the shaking of gourd-rattles. Into this village came Grenville wearing armour, followed by his gentlemen and others in the expedition in corselets and helmets and carrying swords, while the soldiers were equipped with harquebuses and pikes. They must have presented a curious sight to the Indians as they clanked and creaked through the gateway of the palisade and into the area of the camp fire. The sight of them dining would have surprised the Indians even more, as Grenville and his gentlemen ate off ceremonial plate to the sound of music. Unfortunately there is no description of this visit; the journal merely tells us, 'we came to the Towne of Pomeiock'. But John White's drawing shows the village as he found it on 12 July 1585.

From Pomeiooc Grenville went on to visit three other villages up the Pamlico River. As the boats left the Sound with its cooling breeze, it became hotter, and the work of the oarsmen, pulling against the down current of the river, with sweat running into their eyes, became harder. As the English explored the narrow creeks, Indian eyes watched these curious guests from the impenetrable cover of the nearby woods which reached down to the water's edge. The English visited Aquascogoc, Seco and finally the chief village, Secoton.

John White, busy with his brush and pencil, gives us an illustration of Secoton lying on the north side of the Pamlico River (see illustration). Unlike Pomeiooc it is not protected by a palisade. Thirteen huts can be seen, some with their side mats down showing the sleeping benches within, and two huts are all but lost in trees. Three Indians carrying bows are obviously just going hunting. White is anxious to show us the Indian life, and he fills his drawing with activity and interest. Three crops of maize are growing and, set in the ripening corn at top right of his illustration, there is a beehive. In the left foreground is the burial house of the werowances, whose bodies are dried and laid out on a shelf. Above this is the place of solemn prayer, and to the right, across the main axis of the picture, a religious dance is being performed around a circle of eight posts the tops of which are carved with heads. Nine dancers gyrate, shaking gourd-rattles and· seven crouch on the ground – we know they are all men by the feathers in their hair. In the centre of the village three Indians are eating a meal of boiled maize from circular wooden dishes set out on a rush mat.

Grenville was away from Wococon for seven days, returning on 18 July. He covered some 200 miles, a tribute to the stamina of his oarsmen. He explored forty miles up the Pamlico River and established that Core Sound marked the southernmost extent of the Outer Banks. Someone took notes as a basis for a chart of the area – and the party lost a silver cup.

Philip Amadas was sent back to Aquascogoc to collect the cup which, apparently, had been stolen by Indians. But there was more to this episode than the official journal reveals. Amadas, arriving in the village, did not find the cup 'according to promise'. The Indians had wisely fled and the village was deserted, a sound tactic in view of what they knew of the Englishmen's firearms. Amadas' reaction was immediate and brutal; he set fire to all the huts and ruined the surrounding crops. Whatever the Secotan Indians felt about Amadas and his rough justice, it could only have brought joy to Wingina and added to his belief that his new friends were also his allies in tribal warfare.

By the time Grenville returned to Wococon the *Tiger*, with the rest of the fleet, was safely at anchor well clear of the dangerous shoals. Wingina may have sent a welcoming message, for three days later Grenville ordered his ships to weigh anchor and, taking a leisurely seven days, sailed north to Port Ferdinando which lay within sight of Roanoke Island. On 29 July 1585 Granganimeo, still acting as ambassador for his brother, came aboard the *Tiger* with Manteo as interpreter. Reassured by the news of the burning of his enemy's village, Granganimeo made plans and alliances with his new friends in the great cabin over the high stern of the Admiral's ship.

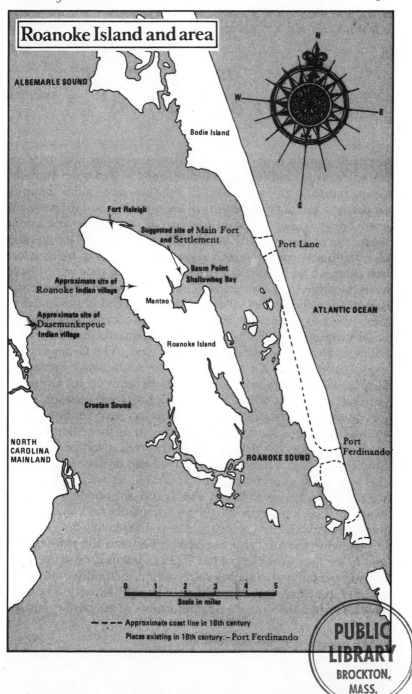

Roanoke Island and area

ALBEMARLE SOUND

Bodie Island

N
W   E
S

Fort Raleigh

Suggested site of Main Fort and Settlement

Port Lane

Baum Point
Shallowbag Bay

Approximate site of Roanoke Indian village

Manteo

ATLANTIC OCEAN

Approximate site of Dasemunkepeuc Indian village

Roanoke Island

Crostan Sound

NORTH CAROLINA MAINLAND

Port Ferdinando

ROANOKE SOUND

0   1   2   3   4   5
Scale in miles

– – – – Approximate coast line in 16th century

Places existing in 16th century:—Port Ferdinando

7

'Brick and Tiles for Fort and Houses'

Grenville's prime concern now was to secure a safe land-base for his colonists with the help of the friendly Roanoke Indians. Granganimeo's priority was to see his new allies happily established and not have them sail away as they had the previous year. They had a common interest and no doubt their discussions went agreeably. Grenville had no problem in getting Granganimeo's agreement to allow the colonists to build a fort and camp on the island; but the location of the base would have been the subject of negotiation. The site needed to be sufficiently distant from the Indian village at the north end of the island to allow the two settlements to exist without encroaching on each other's fishing or agriculture; it was evidently essential that the colonists should be self-sufficient in food. Yet Granganimeo would have wanted the settlement to be near enough for him to keep a watchful eye on what his friends were up to. Grenville required the shelter of a harbour for his boats and pinnace, and a fort on the seaward side of Roanoke to face any Spanish attack through the Outer Banks. Although the site of the settlement and its defending fort has never been discovered, it was probably on Shallowbag Bay. The fort could have been on Baum Point and the settlement close by above the beach, in what is now the marshy area between Baum Point and the modern town of Manteo. This site fulfils all the requirements that would have been put forward by Granganimeo and Grenville.*

Following the amicable agreement between the two leaders, and in the four weeks before the *Tiger* sailed on 25 August 1585, leaving behind 107 colonists safely established under Governor Ralph Lane, there was a great deal of feverish activity. The fleet, now seven in number, rode uncomfortably at anchor beyond the

*See Appendix II for discussion of the site.

lines of breaking Atlantic rollers. The look-outs would have been watching constantly for dragging anchors whenever the northeast breeze freshened, threatening to run the ships onto the beach. The distance to the colony through the surf, over the bar and into the Sound, would have been five miles or more and the ferrying to and fro of the heavily loaded boats in that long haul would have been tough work in the August heat. On days when there was heavy surf – which was frequently – the boats came through the surf safely due only to the skill of the helmsman who caught the crest of a wave at the right moment and surfed in through the Banks while the oarsmen kept the boat stern on to the seas. An inexperienced hand at the helm could easily have let a boat be turned broadside on to the sea causing the gunwales to go under the next wave crest and the boat to be swamped. There was a continuous procession of heavily loaded boats surfing into the Sound, riding the waves in a flurry of flying spray, and bringing in stores for the colony: baggage, tools for skilled tradesmen, lead and iron, equipment, arms, powder, heavy cannon, and the livestock – pigs, horses, cows and poultry.

The first priority of the colonists was to construct temporary shelter, and something was erected on Bodie Island by the entrance to the Sound, presumably acting as a half-way depot from which Lane could oversee the operation. But on Roanoke Island the priority would have been to build the fort and a chapel for daily prayers. Now that there was, after long weeks of comparative idleness, a task for the colonists to perform – a task they had been planning for a year – the burst of excitement in the colony must have been something like the release of a cork from a bottle. Carpenters set to with saws and adzes, smiths with their anvils, and others started felling trees for the fort. The woods nearby were cleared so as to leave an open area allowing no cover for an enemy.

By mid-August the fort was completed and the colonists could then turn their attention to building houses. Since no trace of anything resembling a house has been discovered on Roanoke one can only speculate on what they would have been like. It is inconceivable that the colonists would have constructed anything other than the simple traditional dwellings which had been built and would continue to be built in England for centuries. All the colonists had known and lived in such homes and there would have been no problems in erecting them.

One of the soldiers, Darby Glande was, in a later expedition in 1587, left behind at Mosquetal Bay and consequently captured by the Spaniards. In his interrogation by Spanish authorities he recalled the time when the settlement was being established on Roanoke Island in 1585: 'as soon as they had disembarked they began to make brick and tiles for fort and houses'. Hariot too mentions bricks, but his is not an illuminating reference: 'Now for Stone, Bricke and Lime, thus it is. Heere the Sea Coast where we dwelt, there are no kinds of stone'. After rambling on at length about the unfortunate lack of stone, he mentions that there was clay for making bricks, also that lime for lime mortar and plaster could be made by burning shells. He does not, however, imply that either process had been attempted.

The manufacture of brick at Roanoke would not have been difficult, taking only a few days. The clay would have been discovered and dug out, perhaps by the German miners included in the colony. Successful brickmaking required two sorts of clay: one plastic and doughy, the other sandy and friable (the latter prevents the shrinkage of the former). The colonists only had the sandy, unstable mix. With the 'dough' 'puddled' to remove impurities, the clay would have been stamped out using wooden moulds and set to dry in the hot sun. At Roanoke, in August, the drying process would have taken no more than a week to ten days, followed by firing in a kiln for twenty-four hours. By mid-August they could have had a limited quantity of poor quality bricks, but no tiles could have been produced with the sandy mix of clay.

The statement by Darby Glande has been proved to be partly correct. In the ditch at the Fort Raleigh site a fragment of one brick in poor material made from local sandy clay has been found. In another part of the ditch a fragment of tile has been uncovered. The brick is certainly sixteenth-century and made locally, but whether by the 1585 colony or the later settlers it is impossible to know. On Glande's evidence the brick could date from Lane's 1585 colony. The tile, however, was not made from local clay and must have been imported, most likely by the later settlers, after it had been discovered by Lane that it was impossible to manufacture tiles on Roanoke. Glande, after all, only said that 'they began to make brick and tiles'; he did not say that the tile making was successful.

The bricks would have been used for the foundations of the houses and for fireplaces to heat the dwellings in winter. The tradition in house-building was to prepare a foundation of a stone or brick plinth for the outer and inner walls to stand on. Upon this plinth were laid sill-beams, the horizontal base of a timber frame. On the sill-beams were erected the four corner posts of a cruck. or post-and-truss dwelling. The cruck was a simpler construction than the post-and-truss and was suitable for a small cottage. The four corner posts of a cruck cottage were curved and joined overhead forming a Gothic arch at each end of the frame. The two arches were held and joined by horizontal tie-beams and a roof-ridge at the apex of the arches. At intervals down the side walls vertical posts were let into the sill and tie-beams, the spaces between them being filled with split laths plastered over with mud and daub. The roof was thatched (at Roanoke with reed). This traditional form of construction would have provided a single-room dwelling – exactly like the medieval hall house – in which all activity, cooking, eating and sleeping, was carried on. To one end of the hall would have been a large open fireplace backed with brick. The smoke would have been funnelled up into the roof space by a hood of timber and daub, then left to find its way out through the thatch or by vents in the gable ends. Some houses had two storeys and these are likely to have been of the more complicated post-and-truss construction with more than one room on the ground floor.

The inspiration and driving force behind the creation of the first English settlement in America was undoubetdly its governor, Ralph Lane. Of Lane very little is known. Like many intrepid men he had no imagination, and so could never imagine the worst. To our cost we know that he had great difficulty in expressing himself in writing; the muddled way in which he presented his account of the colony in *Discourse on the First Colony* demonstrates this weakness. However, he was a good leader who inspired loyalty and love and he succeeded at Roanoke when many would have failed. Lane was a courtier and a soldier, having held a minor court post as Equerry of the Great Stable and being knighted in 1593. He had been involved in seafaring in 1571 when Elizabeth had commissioned him to intercept Breton shipping to search for illegal cargoes. He planned a number of expeditions to Spain and Africa which came to nothing (his plans were sometimes unrealistic) and, like so many on the Roanoke venture, he had served in Ireland with the army for two years from 1583 to 1585. He would return again to Ireland in 1592, to remain until he was severely wounded in 1595. He was muster-master on Drake's expedition to Portugal in 1589 and held a similar position the following year on Hawkins' expedition to the Azores. He died in Dublin in 1603.

Lane may have been the son of Sir Ralph Lane of Glendon Hall at Horton in Northamptonshire, who had married a cousin of Katherine Parr, Henry VIII's last wife. Of his appearance nothing is known since no portraits have survived. As an organiser he was not afraid to take decisions and to see them carried out, exercising a soldier's belief in discipline. Inclined to be ruthless, he was not misplaced as the first English governor in America.

While Lane was organising the landing of the stores and the building of the fort, Amadas was sent out on 2 August 1585 to explore and chart the Albemarle River, going up its tributary, the present Perquimans River, as far as the Indian village of Weopemeoc. Journeying through creeks thick with green forest undergrowth overhanging the water, spied on by unseen Indian eyes, Amadas covered a total distance of around 130 miles, and was gone for over a month. In addition to wishing to chart the rivers, he had political motives for making the trip. The Weopemeoc tribe under chief Okisko (Ceremonial Fox), was independent of Wingina and had not been involved in the wars three years ealier. Grenville, no doubt, wished to have Okisko as a peaceful ally and Amadas had time enough to spend as much as ten days with Okisko. By 8 September or earlier, but certainly after the *Tiger* had sailed, Amadas was back at Roanoke Island. The notes he took on this expedition completed a rough chart of the area (see illustration): 'Fresh water with great store of fish' is marked up the Albemarle river on its right bank; on its other bank 'here were great store of great red grapis veri pleasant'. These are the large sweet Muscadine grapes which ripen in September with a flavour quite unlike any European grape; they are, as Amadas said, ' veri pleasant'.

Three days after Amadas set out up the Albemarle River,

John Arundell set sail for England to take the first news of the new colony, in the fastest vessel – one of the prizes taken in the West Indies. He set his mainsail and, with chanting sailors turning the capstan, weighed anchor. With more sail set he was soon away over the eastern horizon bound for England. Carried swiftly across the Atlantic by the westerlies, he arrived some time in early October. The date of his arrival is uncertain, but he was knighted at Richmond on 14 October as bearer of the first intelligence of the Virginian colony to England. He brought news of the near loss of the *Tiger* and the complete loss of her valuable stores, and an urgent request for supplies to replace what had perished; he told of the establishment of the settlement, the building of the fort and the peaceful association with Granganimeo and his tribe. But for those who had hoped that Roanoke could be used as a safe harbour for a plundering fleet, Sir John Arundell could only report that a fleet would get a great welcome from the colonists but it would have to anchor unsafely off the Atlantic shore. One of the principal objectives of the expedition had not been achieved.

Back at Roanoke Island, Governor Lane could, nevertheless, congratulate himself. It was with a sense of considerable achievement that he looked on the small settlement nestling on this American shore close to the protective fort, its colonists existing peacefully with the Indians whose country it was.

8

'Port Ferdinando in Verginia'

As Lane was settling in at his winter quarters, the *Lion*, and the *Dorothy* under Captain Raymond, having dropped thirty men on Croatoan Island around 17 June, had broken all contact with the main expedition and sailed to Newfoundland. They apparently deserted Grenville at the very time when they would have been most needed, but were obviously acting according to a pre-arranged plan. This northern cruise is a curious business and its purpose, which was never explained, can only be guessed at.

By sailing for Newfoundland they could have been following one of the usual routes for England, but for decades Newfoundland had been a base for ships fishing the Banks from April to September. The catch included whale and walrus for their oil, herring, but chiefly cod which, dried and salted, provided a winter diet for Europe when fresh food was a rarity. Fishing was a tough and hazardous occupation, and the French, English and Spanish generally forgot their national differences in this northern no-man's-land, in the common effort to survive. It is likely that the *Lion* and the *Dorothy* had been sent to trade for fish to supplement the diet of the new colony through the winter, perhaps replacing some of what had been lost in the *Tiger*. If this was the case, then Captain Raymond quickly forgot his mission.

In Europe the war with Spain had taken a more serious turn, not so much due to diplomacy, as to one of those acts of God which are unavoidable. By the end of the winter of 1584/5 Spain was suffering the effects of a bad harvest and grain was in desperately short supply. Philip, regarding England as an enemy to all catholics, met the problem by seizing the English grain ships unlucky enough to be lying in Spanish ports. This had taken place on 19 May 1585, after Grenville had sailed; no one in Virginia could have been aware of what had happened. The news of the seizures had reached England in a dramatic manner.

One intrepid captain escaped from Spain with his cargo intact, bringing with him not only a copy of the order but the high Spanish official responsible for the seizures. Queen Elizabeth could not have asked for a more reliable report and, as it turned out, although Lane and his colonists were geographically isolated from the immediate effects of Philip's action, they were not immune to them.

The *Golden Royal* had, in April 1585, begun fitting out for 'Wingan de Coy . . . for taking Spanish ships and those of the subjects of the King of Spain'. Ralegh later explained, 'When some of my people asked the name of the Countrie Roanoke, one of the Savages answered *Wingandacon* which is to say, as you wear gay clothes'.[1] Therefore the *Golden Royal*, fitting out for 'Wingan de Coy', was bound for Roanoke Island and intending to use the colony as a privateering base 'for taking Spanish ships'. The ship was owned by Bernard Drake, a kinsman of Sir Francis Drake on his father's side and of Grenville on his mother's.

After Philip's seizure of the grain ships the plans for the *Golden Royal* were abruptly changed. No longer was she bound for Roanoke. On 20 June Elizabeth commissioned the ship to sail for Newfoundland to protect English interests and to capture whatever Spanish vessels she encountered. Compensating Ralegh for what was mistakenly seen as a less profitable voyage, the Queen made over to him her share in the *Golden Royal*, an investment of £120. With a pressed crew Bernard Drake sailed within ten days.

On the passage out Drake captured his first prize, a Portuguese loaded with sugar. The ship was sent back to England under a prize crew. When he made St John's it is likely that Drake received reports of the *Lion* and the *Dorothy*, for he shortly met up with them in Bay Bulls. Then like a pack of hunting wolves, the three ships, with other vessels now 'consorting' with them, set out to execute the second part of the Queen's commission: to capture Spanish shipping. Whatever had brought Captain Raymond and his two vessels to Newfoundland was now sacrificed for the greater fun and profit of privateering. In Newfoundland no less than sixteen fishing vessels were taken. Then the small fleet headed for the Azores and created havoc amongst Spanish supply lines. Three Brazil-men heavy with cargoes of sugar, wine, gold and elephant ivory, bound for Portugal, were taken; the ivory had been taken to the West Indies by African slavers. The English ships also took a Frenchman coming from Guinea carrying wines and gold. Somewhere on the plundering route they met up with another of Ralegh's ships, the *Job*, carrying sixteen tons of cedar to England – from Roanoke perhaps.

All in all it was a profitable venture for Drake and Ralegh. They lost the profit of the *Job*, its cargo and the Portuguese prizes, when bad weather forced them to shelter in a Breton port and the French impounded the lot. But the remainder of the valuable prizes got to England safely. Drake was knighted at Greenwich on 9 January 1586, but his glory and new wealth were short lived; by 10 April he had died of fever caught from the prisoners he had taken on the voyage.

Back at Roanoke, Grenville was preparing, with the council's approval, to leave for England. The council had agreed that a limited number of colonists – fifteen gentlemen and eighty-two men under Governor Ralph Lane – should remain behind. They would remain on Roanoke until Grenville could return with more stores and colonists. It was never intended that the remaining group should be more than a holding party confirming Ralegh's possession under his royal patent. None of them was granted land and the organisation of the colony was military.

Although the hierarchy was based on military discipline, within the group were some who, by their skills, were there to gather scientific information. Thomas Hariot was one; Joachim Ganz, another, who was expert in smelting copper, and far more than a mere smith; Hans Walters possibly, a surgeon; John White, the scientific observer and artist; and there were also Germans skilled in mining. Ralegh had been advised to include masons, carpenters, an alchemist, an apothecary, as well as farmers; and no doubt many of those listed in the roll-call of the colonists had these skills.[2] Indeed, the colony could not have survived at all, or only with difficulty, without smiths and carpenters.

Lane took the opportunity of sending at least three letters with Grenville on the *Tiger*: two to Walsingham and one to Sir Philip Sidney, all dated 12 August and addressed from 'Port Ferdinando in Verginia'. This was Port Ferdinando, on the northern tip of Hatarask Island, now part of Bodie Island, where Lane was supervising the transfer of supplies and the building of the fort on Roanoke Island.

Lane's first letter to Walsingham was very short and merely tells of the other letter being sent at the same time by a different bearer. The second letter is more interesting. Walsingham was told of the problems of the coast, the shallow access to the Sound being only twelve feet at Port Ferdinando at high water. But, Lane claimed in this letter, the harbour was the best to be found on the coast. In writing that Lane was either being deliberately untruthful or was concealing a compromise. Chesapeake Bay to the north was a far better anchorage and would have made a more strategic base for attacking Spanish shipping, but Lane had not yet explored the area, he only knew of it, and there was, too, the problem of the hostile Chesapeake Indians. At Roanoke, for all its shortcomings as a base for shipping, there was – at least for the moment – the support of friendly Indians. And Roanoke was, of course, the base chosen by Fernandez of whom Lane gives a glowing account. Lane and Fernandez were both Walsingham's men, and it was a case of the team working together. In defending Fernandez' record, Lane was counteracting Grenville's expected charge that the pilot was incompetent and responsible for the grounding of the *Tiger*. There is, in fact, no shred of evidence that Fernandez was at fault.

Grenville and Fernandez were plainly incompatible and had made uncomfortable shipmates in the simmering relationships aboard. That Fernandez was an excellent pilot was acknowledged, but his constant bragging was tedious to Grenville, who himself exacerbated their poor relationship by being an unsatisfactory leader. Lane blamed Grenville for the late arrival at Roanoke 'thoroughe ye default of him yt intendeth to accuse others . . .'. At this stage though, he was only giving subtle hints to Walsingham – he was to be more outspoken in a later letter – perhaps because there was a very good chance that Grenville would read Lane's letters once they were taken on his ship. It must have been galling for Lane to remain in Virginia knowing that Grenville would, on his arrival in England, present his version of events and blacken the reputations of those opposed to him. Did Grenville know of Lane's hostility, or had Lane successfully concealed his feelings? For the future peace and success of the venture Lane would have done best to dissemble, but it was probably beyond him!

Lane was to be left with only small ship's boats and the

pinnace, the latter being the largest vessel which could be used in the Sound and on the rivers and creeks adjoining it. A wooden slipway was built for small boats on Hatarask Island at Port Ferdinando, which was later found by a Spanish party searching for the suspected English base – but by then the settlement was deserted.

Preparations went on for the departure of all the ships: they needed their water casks filling, repairs to rigging and hull, and fresh provision of local fruit and fish taken aboard. By 25 August 1585 Grenville in the *Tiger* was ready to leave. His ship was provisioned, letters taken on board, and what stores he could spare had been given to Lane. Goodbyes had been said and last messages sent to those at home in England. Grenville sailed from Virginia in uneasy partnership with Fernandez as pilot. Lane and his men, with the crews of the smaller ships still to sail, were left on the wide, sandy shore of Hatarask watching the *Tiger*'s sails retreat into the vast Atlantic until they were eclipsed by the line of the eastern horizon.

The building of the settlement went on, for with all the stores now landed there was nothing to hold up the work. And it is likely that the remaining ships were detained while they were careened on the beach. Lane could have felt only relief that Grenville had gone, a relief touched with concern about what sort of case would be made against him in England. But with Grenville and Fernandez departed the tension had gone. Lane was in command of the colony and its destiny was in his hands. He now took the opportunity to write more long letters to send with the departing ships. This time he was not constrained by the possibility of Grenville reading them. On 3 September, having transferred his headquarters across the Sound to Roanoke Island, he wrote his first letter 'From the new Fort in Virginia' – a title which had a triumphant ring. No doubt he wrote sitting beneath the shelter of a new reed thatch inside the newly built fort, occasionally breaking off from his letter to give orders to one of his men. Outside he could probably hear the noise of carpenters' saws, the dull sound of mallets on chisels, the sharper clang of smiths hammering red-hot iron, and distant shouts.

For the first time in weeks Lane could relax. His first letter was to Richard Hakluyt the elder, who had given so much encouragement and useful advice. Lane described what grew in the new land and how it might be exported with advantage. He mentioned 'Guinie wheate' (now called maize or corn), the underdeveloped land which the Indians were incapable of exploiting, the good nature of the inhabitants, and the possibility of selling cloth to them – all these details were of interest to Hakluyt. Lane carefully omitted to mention the grave disadvantages of the area.

Lane's second letter, written four days later, was to Walsingham and also addressed from the new fort. He could now afford to tell the truth as he saw it. He stressed the good record of those whom he knew Grenville would attack. As an example of Grenville's quick temper and manner, he recounted an occasion when, in open council, he had suggested some measure and Grenville had threatened to put him on trial 'for my lyfe' which gives a vivid indication of the tension between the two leaders. Lane then itemised the errors of judgement made by Grenville. With this weight off his mind, he then described the Indians' green corn festival, which he had witnessed in August, and which White illustrated (see illustration).

Lane prefaced his letter by assuming that Grenville would have already arrived in England and made his complaints to both Walsingham and Ralegh. But he was wrong, for Grenville had been delayed.

As the *Tiger* sailed away from Virginia, those on board watched the low coastline vanish into the sea, leaving disjointed trees and hills suspended, shimmering above the water until those, too, disappeared behind the waves. Fernandez now set course for Bermuda. As they held this east-south-easterly course, 1000 miles to the south a Spanish *flota* was assembling in Havana. It comprised thirty-three ships loaded with the valuable produce of the Spanish Empire. Its destination was Spain and it, too, was on a course for Bermuda.[3] The speed of any convoy is that of the slowest ship, and even with a good wind pushing them forward the vast Spanish galleons moved through the water sluggishly. After leaving Havana they ran into foul weather and one, the *Santa Maria de San Vincente*, of around 400 tons, was forced to heave-to by the gale-force winds. She lay all of one night in the trough of the sea with sails furled. It would have been an abominably uncomfortable night, for such vessels with a large beam-to-length ratio roll heavily, and no one would have had any sleep at all. With the coming of first light only six or seven ships of the original *flota* could be seen far ahead in the grey, wet dawn. Putting on as much sail as they dared the captain of the straggler tried to catch up but was unable to do so and as the day progressed he had the frustration of watching his companions disappear in the direction of Spain, leaving the *Santa Maria* alone in the heaving Atlantic at the mercy of any privateer who might come upon her.

Holding the same course, the *Santa Maria* was abeam of Bermuda by 4 September. So too was Grenville in the *Tiger*. With a sharp look-out the Spaniards should have seen the *Tiger* first – maybe they did. At ten o'clock that morning they sighted a white sail following and, foolishly assuming it to be friendly, they let the strange sail catch up with them. As the unknown ship slowly came up with the *Santa Maria*, the Spaniards fired a friendly salute. The *Tiger* had all the classic advantage of the wind, and the enemy, to leeward, was at her mercy. But mercy was far from Grenville's mind while prize money was there for the taking. With decks cleared for action, and bearing down on the enemy, taking all the wind from the *Santa Maria*'s sails, the *Tiger* fired a broadside straight into the Spaniard. The crew was outmanoeuvred and taken completely by surprise. They had made every mistake and were easy prey to the skilful Fernandez. The Spaniards were even unequipped with arms to defend themselves against the boarding party which they knew must follow. The *Tiger* had fired her cannon partly to disable the enemy by cutting through the rigging and partly to hole the hull. By the time the Spaniards realised their mistake it was too late to get away. One man had been killed and four or five others injured. Their ship lay-to in a cross-sea, her rigging in a tangled disorder, hanging over the side; with every roll, seawater slopped and flooded through two black splintered holes in her side. Wallowing in the heavy swell the Spaniards watched while the *Tiger* organised a boarding party. The ship's boat had been left with Lane at Roanoke Island so 'a boat made with boards of chests' was pressed into service. Over the side went thirty-six soldiers, Grenville, as General, leading the boarding party. Those aboard the *Santa Maria* watched fearfully as the soldiers awkwardly rowed their craft across the water separating the two ships. Then the drama turned to farce: the boat moved slower and slower – it was making water – it was sinking! Grenville, urging on the oarsmen, could see that they might not make the side of the Spaniard, but he felt at a serious disadvantage, not knowing that the Spaniards had no firearms to defend themselves. Those aboard the *Santa Maria* watched this turn of fortune with pleasurable interest, until Grenville and his boarding party arrived alongside the towering bulk of their victim. As their unreliable craft disintegrated in the sea, they scrambled aboard.

Grenville at once ordered the master, passengers and others to hand over gold, silver and jewellery as well as items totalling over 20,000 ducats entered in the ship's register. Keeping his thirty-six men, Grenville sent twenty of the Spanish seamen to the *Tiger* as hostages, leaving a bare twenty-two Spanish sailors and passengers. He was taking no chances of being outnumbered but was cutting it a bit fine to expect so few seamen to sail the ship. Provisions were transferred to the *Tiger*, where food was running short, and, with damage made good, the two ships set course for England.

But the dramas were not yet over; within days another storm blew up, separating the two vessels. Grenville kept steadfastly on course for home, impressing his Spanish prisoners by dining off silver and gold plate to a musical accompaniment – the trammels of his rank displayed ashore were maintained on board ship. Supplies of food ran low, so low that the ration was reduced to a few oats a day cooked in salt water: it had been a mistake to transfer so many provisions to the *Tiger*. Did Grenville still dine in state? Given the Elizabethan obsession with honour and rank, the likelihood is that Grenville had his boiled oats served on gold plate and still ate to the sound of music. But this grandeur apart, it was hardship for all on board made worse by the stench of a cargo of hides. This was no victorious voyage of triumph: it had become a fight for survival.

On 12 October the island of Flores in the Spanish Azores was sighted and the severe need of supplies now overruled caution.[4] But Grenville had shown cunning in the Caribbean on the voyage out and now, in the extreme of necessity, showed it again. As the *Santa Maria* slowly approached land, Grenville ordered all his men to keep out of sight and to make no sound. Only the passengers and the Spanish crew were allowed to be seen – no doubt covered by the pistols of Grenville's soldiers. From the small boats which came out to escort the ship in to an anchorage,

Grenville, with cool assurance, seized five boatmen as hostages, not to be released until supplies were delivered. This the islanders refused to do. Finally one of the Spanish passengers was sent ashore to convince officials that his twenty-one fellow passengers would be thrown overboard to drown or be eaten by sharks unless supplies of food were quickly delivered. This strong message succeeded and supplies of desperately needed food, drinking water and fuel for cooking were sent. In return most, but not all, of the hostages were released, and the rest were carried on to England.

Grenville made Plymouth on 18 October 1585 and Ralegh was one of the first to visit his returned general, to get a personal account of the venture. Grenville's first concern, however, was to secure his valuable prize against pilferage, and he was still detained at Plymouth when he wrote to Walsingham on 29 October. Ralegh, by this time, had returned to London and the court, no doubt taking with him Lane's two letters addressed to Walsingham. Walsingham had already received Lane's later and more revealing letters so critical of Grenville. Now Grenville wrote a letter to Walsingham which eventually must have convinced the Secretary of State that Grenville was not to be trusted. In this letter he blandly informed Walsingham that the value of the *Santa Maria* and the cargo was a mere £12,000 to £15,000, whereas the registered value of the cargo alone was in the region of £50,000. Grenville was cheating his associates!

Given the substantial value of the prizes taken, investors in the Virginian venture received a good return and this was fine publicity for the relief expedition.

The purpose of the whole venture had been, so far, a secret kept from Spain, but the prisoners released from the *Santa Maria* in Flores had given Spanish authorities their first news – exaggerated and incorrect – of the English colony: 300 men and five warships on the Florida coast! Menéndez Marqués, the Spanish Governor of Florida in San Agustín, so long delayed in his return to Spain, now had a real cause for concern and a pressing reason to scour the Florida coast. Little did he know that the following year the evidence of the English in America would be violently presented to him on his very doorstep.

9

'Contrarie to all Expectation'

With the departure of Grenville for England in August 1585, Lane, previously styled 'General' and therefore in charge of military matters only, assumed the fuller title of Governor which effectively extended his authority over all activities within the new colony. Lane's second-in-command was Philip Amadas, who, in 1585, was just twenty-one. His family was from Plymouth and he was related to both the Hawkinses and Arthur Barlow. Amadas retained his title of Admiral, which meant that he had command of the pinnace and the boats. The command of the military side of the colony was shared between Captains Edward Stafford and John Vaughan, who each had under him fifty men, comprising a company. These two captains effectively commanded the land-based operations.

There is little mention of the social hierachy within the colony (it was so self-evident at the time as to need no comment), but there is no reason to suspect that the colonists departed from the customs they knew at home in England. Theirs would have been a military organisation, but the title of Governor has a civic ring to it. No doubt this was to allow the scientific activities of Hariot, of White and the metal experts, to be included in Lane's command.

The houses of the settlement would have varied in consequence according to the rank of the occupant. Governor Lane would have had the largest in the colony, a two-storey dwelling, complete with a central hall for his attendants to eat and sleep in. To one end of the hall would have been a parlour for Lane to work in and to receive less important visitors; above it a chamber for receiving more important visitors and for Lane to eat and sleep in; and to the other end of the hall would have been the kitchen, buttery and pantry. Lane's rank and consequent style of living, necessary to impress the Indians and the lesser ranks of the colonists, would not have allowed cooking in the hall.[1]

Amadas, as Admiral, would have occupied something less grand, and the two captains probably shared one dwelling equal in size to that of Philip Amadas. How the other gentlemen were accommodated can be the subject of only the vaguest speculation. Hariot and White would have had their own quarters. Others, if they were not attached to the households of Lane, Amadas, Hariot or White, might even have their own hearths. But for the majority privacy, either ashore or afloat, was an unknown luxury, and there would have been no question of the ninety-odd colonists who were not gentlemen having their own houses. They would have slept in communal guardhouses or the halls of their superiors.

There would have been storehouses for provisions and other essential supplies, whilst the powder and munitions would have been stored inside the fort, where there was also a jail. A smithy and a carpenter's shop would have been essential to the colony, as well as a saw-pit for cutting planks. A cookhouse is also a likely provision, for the lesser ranks would have needed catering for as on board ship. All in all, even for these few basic requirements, the settlement would have needed numerous structures to accommodate the new colony.

What Lane and his colonists were doing during the autumn and winter of 1585 is not clear. Lane's account is only detailed, in a muddled way, from 1586 until the time the colony left Roanoke Island. It was during this early period that the sconce at the north end of the island must have been built, but Lane makes no mention of this. The Indians generously allocated maize crops on the mainland for the English; beer was brewed which must have improved morale immensely, but what effect the beverage had on the Indians is something else about which Lane is silent. He does tell us, however, that the Indians, and even Wingina, joined the colonists at prayer in the chapel.

In the autumn of 1585 a party of exploration was sent northwards up the coast, bound for Chesapeake Bay in the charge of an anonymous 'Colonel of the Chesepians' – perhaps Stafford or even Hariot. The party followed the Sound north until it petered out in narrows and shallows, then followed the sea coast up to Cape Henry at the mouth of Chesapeake Bay. Here the explorers passed the winter at Chesepuic, the principal village of the Chesepian tribe. A defensive fort was built (another site ignored by archaeologists!). Chesapeake provided a far better harbour than Roanoke Island and, after the party returned, Lane recognised its value. He proposed making the main settlement on the Bay as soon as the relief supplies with more colonists arrived.

The danger facing settlement on Chesapeake was the Indians' hatred of Europeans, inspired by the ruthless reprisals taken in 1572 by the Spanish after the extermination of the Jesuit mission. The friendly reception accorded to Lane's party of exploration is accounted for by the fact that the Chesepian Indians had not been involved in the earlier trouble. It was the tribes of what later became known as the Powhatan Confederacy which had suffered the Spanish reprisals, and the Chesapians did not belong to the Powhatan group of tribes. During the explorers' winter sojourn at the Indian village of Chesepuic, neighbouring kings or werowances came to talk with the Englishmen. These werowances were from tribes living inland further to the west of Chesapeake – the Tripanicks, the Oppossians and the Iroquoi – who all formed part of a loose alliance which became the basis of the Powhatan Confederacy. Here was a chance for the Powhatan tribes to annihilate half of Lane's colony, but they did not seize it. The intricacies of Indian politics now escape us, but it looks as though Wingina had an alliance with these tribes and it was his influence which preserved the English explorers. Wingina would shortly change his policy.

The exploration completed, the 'Colonel of the Chesepians' led his men, carrying their boats with them, overland to the head of the Sound. They arrived back at Roanoke about February. It is infuriating that Lane in his account published in 1589 by Hakluyt in *Principal navigations* tells so little about this very important northern probe which must have influenced the eventual site of the later Jamestown settlement. However, the lack of detail is deliberate; to have told everything would have revealed too much to the Spaniards.

We are left in the dark also about the personal relationships between the colonists and the Indians. Can one believe that out of a party of over 100 men who had seen no women for nine months there was no one who fraternised with the Indians? Hariot denies it; Lane is silent on the matter (at least he does not attempt to convince us that his discipline was so successful as to prevent any of his men taking Indian mistresses); and it is reported that the Indians were surprised at this lack of interest. Neither does Lane make any mention of Indian marriage customs. One of White's drawings is entitled 'one of the wives of Wingina' and the Jamestown colonists found that the Indians were polygamous;[2] therefore there is no reason to suspect that Wingina's people were not. Did some of Lane's men live with several women in happy concubinage? If they did, then the attempt to turn Roanoke into a garden of Eden would have been a source of friction between the two cultures. Perhaps Hariot is telling the truth when he says, astonishingly, that nothing went on. For one thing, as soon as the English arrived they were employed on building houses and establishing the settlement. Others were sent exploring and when all this activity had passed the relationship with the Indians had deteriorated into hostility. Did any of the colonists desert the settlement and 'go Indian'? Lane would hardly have admitted as much had it been so, and in the later crisis the Indians would certainly have killed any lone Englishman. These intriguing details of Lane's occupation of Roanoke Island can be supplied only by imagination.

By the time the colonists had at last settled in on Roanoke, it was too late to plant crops; this was the reason for Wingina's generous gift of ripe crops of corn. They did, however, have sheep, pigs and cattle, and could fish and hunt. For the present the flour stocks, such as remained from the disaster with the *Tiger*, provided them with bread, but there inevitably came a time when the colony had to barter with the Indians for maize and other food. The Roanoke Indians, being few more than the total number of colonists, were not able to support the demands made on their stocks, however much they coveted the knives and copper they could get in exchange. As supply dwindled through the winter, so friction arose between the colony and the Indians. Wingina was disappointed in the hope that his English friends would support him in a new war against his enemies, the Secotans, in the south. As long as the colonists provided their hosts with a valuable service they would be welcome and worth the economic cost of their support; as soon as there was no return for this cost, however, then Wingina would plainly find his guests unwelcome. As the winter drew on this point was reached.

Wingina, although king of his tribe, was not an absolute ruler. He shared his authority with a council of elders or werowances who deliberated on matters concerning the government of the tribe. As in all such councils there were doves and hawks when it came to discussing policy towards the colonists. Some favoured exterminating the colony when they realised that Wingina's plan for enlisting the English as allies had foundered, and they now turned against him. Granganimeo, on the other hand, who had most to do with the colony and who was their nearest neighbour, understandably supported the continuation of friendly relations; it was safer for the survival of his own village. Unfortunately Granganimeo died during the autumn or spring and the balance on Wingina's council of elders was weighted in favour of the hawks and against the colonists. Around the camp fire of the elders the discussion raged until the hawks won the day and no doubt Wingina, too, altered his opinion. It was at this point that Wingina took his 'war name' of Pemisapan (meaning, appropriately, 'He supervises') and it was no longer safe for Lane to trust him.

No hint of the sinister adoption of the 'war name' or of its intent filtered through to Lane or his men. Manteo, who was not of Pemisapan's tribe, certainly knew nothing, and Wanchese, if he knew, said nothing. Life in the settlement went on as usual. We may imagine the fort overlooking the settlement being constantly manned by a look-out and guarded against a surprise attack by Spaniards. Down on the beach minor repairs to boats may have been in hand; colonists went off to visit their fish traps, which the Indians had shown them how to make; the livestock was gradually killed off for food.

After the return of the explorers from Chesapeake, Lane, in March 1586, led a second expedition himself. He was motivated to find a convenient land route to Chesapeake and to discover more about the possibilities of the area so strongly recommended by the recent exploration. Lane chose to take the unwieldy pinnace up the Albemarle River to where the Chowan River runs into the Albermarle. From there, following the Chowan, he went north as far as the river would allow his boats to go. This rather roundabout route was unavoidable if the sea passage was not to be used; the area between the Chowan River and the coast is even now taken up with lakes and swamps known as Dismal

Swamp. In Lane's day this area was unoccupied by Indians and all but inaccessible. It had no strategic value and, yielding no useful minerals or pearls, could safely be ignored.

Lane and his party were navigating the Chowan River. On either bank the forest, growing right down to the water's edge, was never still from the wildlife living in it. The sudden nervous scurry and jump of the grey squirrels set dead leaves rustling on the ground, and the splash of the oars was echoed by the splash of water animals living in the banks. They proceeded in this way through the lands of the Chawanoac tribe until they reached the principal village called Chawanoac, where a surprise awaited them.

Pemisapan, as his name changed from Wingina suggests, had finally decided on an all-out war to destroy the colony. Since this was a task beyond the capabilities of his tribe alone, he had sent messengers to neighbouring tribes telling them of his pretended knowledge of a plan on the part of the colonists to attack them. He suggested an alliance to face the foreigners and defeat them. It was fortunate that the colonists arrived at Chowanoac village that day.

The village lay on a creek set back about a quarter of a mile from the right bank of the river. It may have been the distance from the river which enabled Lane to approach the village unseen (for once the celebrated Indian watchfulness was lacking), for he and his men marched purposefully into the settlement of matted huts, and burst without warning into a full assembly of Indians discussing Pemisapan's proposed alliance against the Englishmen. Chiefs and werowances had converged on the village from the tribes bordering the Albemarle River: the Mangoaks from the west, the Weapemeocs from the east, the Moratucs from the south. There were also of course, the Chawanoacs, under their chief Menatonon (He-listens-carefully), acting as hosts in their own territory.

It was immediately apparent to Lane, by the numbers of Indians sitting on the ground at the open-air assembly, that something was going on. Although he tells us surprisingly little about what followed, his arrival must have been electrifying, spreading consternation, alarm and panic among the Indians, who understandably took his appearance to be magical. Amid the confusion Lane seized Menatonon as his prisoner. This must have been easy because, as the others fled, he was unable to move: he was 'a man impotent in his lims, but otherwise for a savage, a very grave and wise man, and of very good and singular discourse in matters concerning the state'.

With Menatonon in his power, Lane could dominate proceedings. Moreover, during the two days that the unfortunate Indian chief was held in handcuffs by Lane, he told his captor of Pemisapan's plans to attack the colonists, as well as a great deal about the surrounding terrain and sources of pearls and minerals.

Lane learnt that three days' journey by canoe up the Chowan River, then four days' march northwards overland would bring them to a bay where lived on an island a chief who possessed great quantities of pearls. Menatonon went on to tell Lane that this same chief had been at Chawanoac village two years earlier and had given him a string of these very pearls which he in turn gave to Lane. The pearls were certainly very large but all were black. Although pearls in shellfish are a rarity now in Chesapeake, then the Indians found them more commonly in mussels as well as oysters. The blackening came from the Indian practice of cooking the shellfish before opening them. Menatonon also told Lane that up the river Moratuc (the Roanoke) at Chaunis Temoatan were ample supplies of *wassador* – the Indian term for all metals – of the colour of copper or gold.

Lane was questioning Menatonon through Manteo, one of the two Indians who had spent the previous year in England. We can easily imagine Lane, in the gloom of an Indian hut, leaning closer to the old man, his eyes brightening at the name of *wassador* even before Manteo translated the full sentence into English. In his zeal to find precious metals Lane was being realistic: if the colony were to become viable it had to have exports to send back to England in exchange for the supplies the colonists would need. Chaunis Temoatan, Menatonon revealed, was near a salt sea. The name of the place had a magical sound to it – Chaunis Temoatan on the edge of the Pacific Ocean. Lane had little idea of the vast width of America and what he was told seemed very possible.

By now Lane and Menatonon had arranged to take the chief's son Skiko (Seal of the Ocean) as hostage in the old man's place as a guarantee of the peaceful intentions of his tribe. The Indians would have known of Lane's reputation for a brutal reaction when provoked, and the arrangement effectively scotched the hostility organised by Pemisapan – for the moment at least.

Menatonon had told Lane the truth as he knew it and was probably not a party to the treachery that followed. By being false he would have lost his favourite son Skiko. He had never travelled as far as the metal sources and was relying on hearsay and a faulty memory. Pure copper was brought from Lake Superior – Menatonon's salt sea? – and small lodes of copper were found in the Blue Ridge Mountains to the west, where the Roanoke River rose; Menatonon may have been confusing the two. Lane in his anxiety to be certain, cross-checked the information with Skiko. Skiko had once been a prisoner with the Mangoaks whose tribal lands Lane would have to cross to reach Chaunis Temoatan, but he had never been as far as this now fascinating goal. He thought it lay about twenty days overland from the Mangoaks' country.

With this apparently valid information Lane set out immediately for Chaunis Temoatan. With him went forty men in the wherry and another boat he called 'a light horseman'. Menatonon provided guides for one day's travel to the Mangoaks' country. Skiko was taken to Roanoke in the pinnace under heavy guard. Here we must suspect that Menatonon may not have been completely truthful, for he knew very well how far away the Mangoaks' country was and he also knew that Lane only had sufficient food for two days. As Lane said:

> But it fell out very contrarie to all expectation, and likelyhood: for after two dayes travell, and our whole victual spent, lying on shoare all night, wee could never see man, onely fires wee might perceive made alongst the shoare where we were to pass, and up into the countrie untill the very last day. In the evening whereof, about three of the clocke we heard certaine savages call as we thought, Manteo, who was also at that time with mee in the boate.

Lane and his men camped that night on the narrow, high shore of the riverbank. Wisely the party chose to sleep on the boats after posting lookouts. As Lane said, there was a sudden call in the night out of the darkness of the forest, which sounded to him like 'Man-t-e-oo' echoing and re-echoing around them. Then began a war-chant ringing through the trees facing the river, louder and louder; insistently reverberating through the night air. This was

something the English had not experienced before. It was
disconcerting and intimidating to have these strange savage cries
coming at them out of the murky obscurity of the forest. It was
within three days of Easter and the river bank was illuminated by
the light of the almost full moon. As the 'light horseman' made
ready to land men to beat off the attack, and Lane covered the
manoeuvre from the wherry further out in the river, the Indians
burst onto the moonlit shore letting off a volley of arrows into the
nearest boat. The missiles rattled about the boat and off helmets
and corselets but none of the men was hurt. Undeterred, the
landing party made the shore. Encumbered by their heavy
helmets and corselets and carrying their unwieldly firearms, they
lumbered into the forest led by two bull-mastiffs baying loudly in
the excitement of the chase. The animals had been brought over
from England and the Indians were particularly frightened of
these dogs which could bring down a running man. The
attackers, however, knew their own country and had vanished
quickly and effectively; Lane's men found no one.

When Lane had determined to go up the Roanoke River,
Pemisapan had sent word to his neighbours, the Moratucs and
Mangoaks, warning them that Lane intended to attack and
telling them to desert the riverside villages taking with them all
supplies useful to the foreigners. Pemisapan planned to lure the
party so far up the river that supplies would run out and they
would be unable to survive the return journey. The night attack
was a futile gesture which only warned Lane of the danger he was
running into. Manteo, who had spent so long in England, was
considered by the Indians to be a deserter and would not have
been in their confidence; he may also not have known how far
away the Mangoak tribal lands lay. Wanchese, who had been
taken to England with Manteo, had by now deserted and had
rejoined his tribe.

Unshaken by the sudden night attack, Lane took his party of
exploration even further up river the next day but, warned by
events, took more care when camping that night. Lane's resolve
was running out, and so was his food; he and his men supped that
evening off the two bull-mastiffs cooked in sassafras leaves.
Indeed it was time to turn back! Next morning he and his men
agreed to go no further and to return to Roanoke Island. They
were about 100 miles up river. It had taken them three days' hard

rowing against the current, and so would take less time running down. But even when clear of the river there was still some distance to cover in the Sound before they came to Chepanoc, a Weapemeoc village on the north shore of the Albemarle Sound, where Lane felt certain they would find friendly Indians to give them food. Lane made clear to his men the desperate situation they were in: two days' supply of food only and 140 miles to cover before they could hope to find more!

Spurred on by their predicament, they made very good time down the river and arrived in the Sound that night, camping on what is now called Sans Souci Island in the river mouth. They ate hungrily off boiled sassafras leaves – there was no dogmeat left – aromatic and tough; the root was considered a cure for venereal disease. The following day, Saturday and Easter eve, there was a very strong wind blowing against them in the Sound, whipping up waves which threatened to swamp both boats. Discretion ruled, and rather than risk being drowned Lane chose to remain in the safety of Sans Souci, facing a less certain end by starvation. Lane made the nearest he ever came to a joke when he referred to the appropriateness of a fast over Easter. Easter day came, 3 April. The storm had blown itself out, the Sound was calm, and they were on their way again. By the time the forty miles to Chepanoc were covered, the men in the smaller boat were in a bad way. The Indian village was deserted; the visitors had been seen only shortly before, and the vanished Indians had left some fish in their hurry, but little else. On the Monday, Lane and his exhausted party at last arrived at the safety of the colony on Roanoke Island. But it was only comparative safety. With the Indian population now against them numbering some 5000, Lane and his colonists had their backs to the wall. They could only survive by outwitting the cunning of the Indians.

10

'A Camvisado'

The safe return of Lane's party astonished Pemisapan. He had not expected to see them again – their survival must be supernatural. No doubt his council met immediately in Dasemunkepeuc, the tribal village on the mainland, sandwiched between Alligator River and the Sound on the edge of the swamps. In the council there was only one who supported the colonists, a werowance called Ensenore. He is a shadowy figure, even the meaning of his name is lost. Lane tells us almost nothing about him except that he was 'a savage father to Pemisapan being the only frend to our nation that we had amongst them'. What Lane meant by 'a savage father' he does not bother to explain. Was Ensenore father-in-law, stepfather, or even foster-father to Pemisapan? Clearly he had great influence in the Indian councils for 'hee alone, had before opposed himselfe in their consultations against all matters proposed against us'. He must have been extremely strong-minded to be able to stand alone in support of the foreigners against all the contrary opinion of his tribal council.

Before the episode of the Roanoke River, Ensenore had suggested that the colonists who came from the ocean were servants of God or Mantoac and could not be destroyed. Another theory was that the colonists were not born of woman and were therefore immortal. A third suggestion was that these strange visitors were transmigrates which again made them immortal. Whatever individual members of the council may have thought they were all – with the one exception of Ensenore – behind Pemisapan in his desire to exterminate them. Ensenore's suggestion that those who attacked the foreigners would suffer, appeared to be coming true. It was thought that the colonists had some way of killing their enemies at a distance for, within days after the Englishmen had visited Indian villages, Indians began to die. They had probably caught measles or the common cold, which can be fatal to those without immunity.

With the return of the party from the Roanoke River, Ensenore's views seemed to be confirmed – for the moment at least. Did not the survival of those who came ashore through a hail of arrows denote some divine interference turning the missiles from them? These foreigners brought metals unknown to the Indians; and none of them had been sick since arrival, whilst the Indians were suffering not only disease but death since coming into contact with colonists. Furthermore, from mid-October to mid-November, just before the serious sicknesses began, a bright comet had appeared in the sky. These men were not like ordinary mortals, for they brought no women with them and they had no interest in the Indian women (difficult to believe but we shall have to take their word for it). There was, too, the special magic of being able to send messages by writing; this amazed many Indians and continued to do so throughout the colonists' stay in Virginia. Whilst all these points appeared convincing to some of the elders, there were others more sceptical: 'These strangers consume food as ordinary people do and therefore they are not divine beings' was one argument amongst others used against Ensenore. Amongst those ranged against the colonists were Wanchese, who should have been listened to by Ensenore because he had been to England, and two other Indians, Tanaquiny (Many Trees) and Osocan. Both the latter would shortly be actively involved against Lane. For the moment, in the councils held within the dusty village compound, Ensenore had his way; the foreigners, because of their seemingly magical powers, should be treated with respect.

Thanks to Ensenore the colonists were safe from harassment; but it was only to be a short interlude. Whoever the foreigners' gods were, these gods had to be appeased by the Indians. Pemisapan, in propitiation, planted a first crop of spring corn for the colonists and set aside some cleared land for them to plant for themselves. These two gestures on Pemisapan's part would have cost him something in barter for extra seed from a neighbouring tribe and in labour to clear the ground. Although this was a useful and friendly gesture towrds the foreigner-divinities, it did not answer Lane's immediate food problems. The corn would not be ready for harvesting until early July and the Indians' winter

Their rype corne
Their greene corne
Corne newly sprong
Their sitting at meate
The place of solemne prayer
The house wherin the Tombe of their Herounds standeth.
SECOTON.
A Ceremony in their prayers wth strange gestures and songs dansing abowt posts carued on the topps lyke mens faces.

The village of Secotan, by John White

An Indian corn festival, by John White

'The Towne of Pomeiock' in July 1585, by John White

'The manner of their attire and
painting themselves', by John White

Ralegh's Virginia, by John White

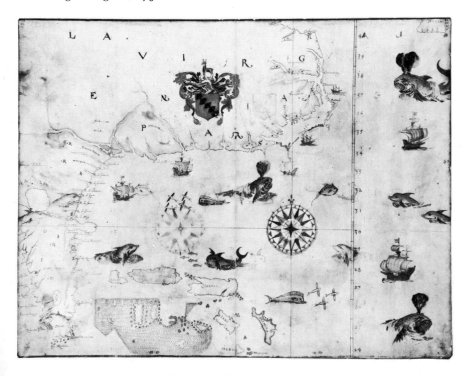

'La Virgenia Pars', by John White. The coast from Chesapeake Bay to Cape Lookout.

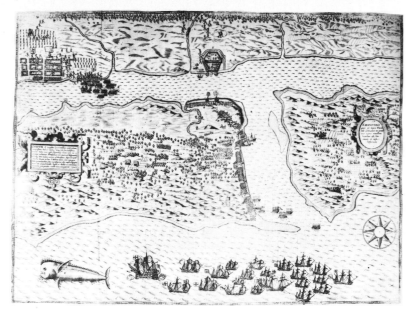

The taking of San Agustín by Drake in May 1586. The fleet is anchored offshore at the bottom of the illustration. In the centre the soldiers are marching up the bank of the river, while, at top centre, the fort guarding the river is being assaulted. At the top left the town is attacked.

May 1585. Grenville's camp at Mosquetal Bay, St John's Island, by John White. The *Tiger* lies at anchor in the bay.

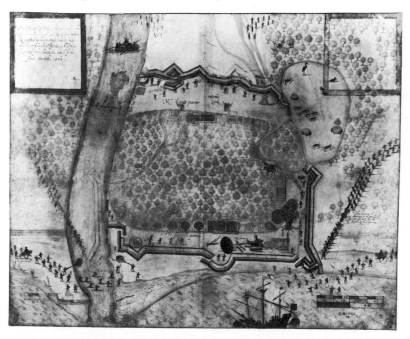

Ralph Lane taking the salt on 26 May 1585, by John White

The Fort Raleigh site at the north end of Roanoke Island

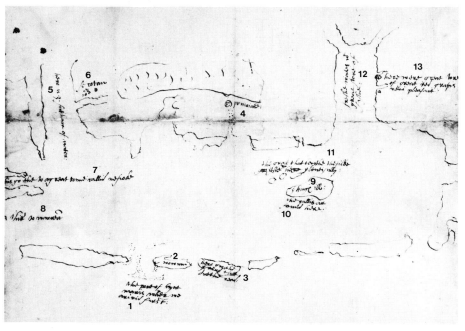

Sketch map of Ralegh's Virginia, September 1585

[1] the port of saynt maris wher we arivid first:
[2] wococan
[3] here groith y^e roots that diethe read:
[4] pomaioke:
[5] here is .3. fatham of water:
[6] secotan
[7] [t]his goithe to a great toune callid nesioke
[8] [   ] this to warreā
[9] ye king*es* ill:
[10] the gallis are found here:
[11] the grase that berither the silke groithe here plentifully:
[12] freshe water *with* great store of fishe:
[13] here were great store of great red grapis veri pleasant:

[*Endorsed:*] A description of the land of virginia

Miniature of Sir Walter Ralegh by
Nicholas Hilliard *c*.1585

Right: Sir Richard Grenville, 1571, by an
unknown artist

Below: Sir Francis Walsingham,
attributed to J. de Critz the elder

Right: Thomas Hariot 1621. A print
after a portrait at Trinity College,
Oxford

stocks of roots, cassada and chyna – used for making bread – were all but used and little could be spared. Lane's concern was how to feed his men until the harvest was ready or the relief ships arrived, whichever came first.

A dramatic gesture was to come from Menatonon (Careful Listener) king of the Chawonoacs, he who was 'impotent in his lims'. Menatonon sent a messenger to visit his son Skiko (Seal of the Ocean), whose imprisonment as hostage had been extended to cover his father's good will for another overland expedition in search of Chesapeake or Chaunis Temoatan. With the messenger came a present of a pearl. Pemisapan explained to Lane that this was intended to be the payment of a ransom for the return of Skiko. Lane therefore refused the gift. Menatonon, however, had commanded Okisko (Ceremonial Fox), king of the Weapemeocs, a dependent tribe living to the east of the Chawanoacs, to offer himself and his tribe in homage to Queen Elizabeth, 'the great Werowanza of England', and Ralegh. With Menatonon's messenger had come twenty-four of Ceremonial Fox's principal men who, before presenting themselves to Lane, had to ask the permission of Pemisapan to carry out Menatonon's bidding – no doubt because the colony was established on Roanoac tribal land. Perhaps this curious sub-division of power was due to some partly forgotten war, or marriage with kings or chiefs. We can begin to understand the difficulties of having no written language: important matters such as this had to be confirmed with each chief with maximum publicity and many witnesses so that all could comprehend the contract.

The whole pageant of the twenty-four Weapemeocs making this journey is an interesting example of the interplay of tribal loyalties. The Indians, tattooed with their tribal marks, their half-naked bodies painted in tribal decoration, wore nothing but the usual fringed deerskin skirt trimmed with a puma tail behind. Around their necks and wrists were ropes of pearls or beads, and their ears were adorned with rings of copper or of bone, or claw of bird. The Weapemeocs, armed with six-foot hazel-wood bows and with two or three feathers stuck in their short hair, canoed the wide Albemarle Sound, a distance of twenty-five miles, much of it out of sight of land. They arrived first at Dasemunkepeuc, the Roanoac tribal village on the mainland, or at the Indian village on Roanoke Island. When the twenty-four Indian braves were received by Lane, we can be sure that he was equal to the occasion and devised some ceremony impressive both to the Indians and the colonists. Lane had every reason to be gratified with events, but his satisfaction was shortlived. On 20 April 1586 he lost his only ally – Ensenore died.

It is ironic that Granganimeo and Ensenore, the two Indians so closely allied to Lane and the colony, probably died because of their association with the foreigners, from infections to which they had acquired no immunity. With Ensenore's influence removed for ever from the councils of Pemisapan, the hawks had their way and a plan to attack the colony was devised. During the winter Pemisapan had been glad to trade food for copper with the colonists; this was now stopped. Earlier the chief had twice been sick and, despairing of the cures of his own medicine men, had sent to the colonists to come and pray by his bed. The foreigners' magic worked: on both occasions Pemisapan had recovered from the contagions brought by his guests. All such friendly exchanges now ceased. The fish weirs assigned to the colonists were wrecked, and food for the colony became scarce. Falling back on an old Indian custom, Lane sent some of his men away to feed themselves on distant islands until the harvest was ready. Twenty men under Stafford were sent to Croatoan to fend for themselves and to watch for the expected relief ships. Master Prideaux was sent in the pinnace to Hatarask (Cape Kenrick) with ten men and the unnamed Provost Marshal to help him; they too were to act as look-outs. Every week sixteen to twenty men were sent in turn to the mainland to grub for cassada and live off oysters. So Lane contrived to feed his men through the lean weeks until the end of June came with the promise of the harvest nearly ready. But this strategy also reduced Lane's immediate fighting strength by around fifty men.

Using the large stocks of copper built up through the winter from bartering with the colony for food, Pemisapan planned to hire 800 warriors from the Mangoaks and Chesepian tribes to supplement the few he could raise from his own Roanoac tribe. The colonists would therefore be outnumbered by about eight to one, although Lane estimated that ten of his own men could defeat a hundred Indians! Pemisapan had been spending most of his time in the Roanoke Indian village but, because Lane had been sending to him daily for supplies of desperately needed food, he soon found the refusing of Lane's messengers less onerous from the further distance of Dasemunkepeuc, his principal tribal village on the mainland, where he took himself – ostensibly to oversee the planting of the second crop. From this point he could also despatch messengers with copper currency to the Mangoaks and Weapemeocs – the Chesepians were no longer involved – without being detected by the colonists. If all the activity of contacting the various distant chiefs and collecting the warriors had been carried out on Roanoke Island it would have been evident to Lane that something unusual was happening. Amongst the 800 warriors, in full war-paint and in high spirits, converging on Dasemunkepeuc there was some dissension: Okisko, chief of the Weapemeocs, remembering his allegiance to the 'Great Werowanza of England' played it both ways. He led his own men away, refusing to take part in the attack, but allowed his lesser werowances and their men to join Pemisapan, so keeping his pact but at the same time receiving the copper payment.

Another disadvantage of having no written language was the difficulty of keeping plans secret: when details had to be conveyed by word of mouth, many not concerned in the matter learned more than they should. Pemisapan managed, however, to keep his manoeuvres secret from Lane until Skiko (Seal of the Ocean) was constrained to tell all he knew. Skiko, Lane's hostage, had tried to escape. He was caught, 'put in the bylboes' – chained to a sliding bar by leg-irons – detained in the gaol house in the fort, and threatened with beheading if he made another attempt. This was in early April, when Pemisapan was making his conciliatory gestures to Lane. Strangely Skiko was given to Pemisapan for safe keeping. Pemisapan then made two mistakes: he treated his prisoner worse than had Lane, and he told him of the plans to eliminate the colony. After Lane's bloodthirsty threats, it is surprising to find that Skiko was more badly treated by the Roanoac king, his own countryman, but as a result of this the prisoner returned to Lane's fort with relief, telling all he knew of Pemisapan's plans. The bad news was shortly confirmed to Lane by one of Pemisapan's men, who was promptly executed by his king; the killing, however, was for another transgression – Permisapan did not suspect that Lane knew of his designs.

Pemisapan had planned that two of his principal men – Tanaquiny (Many Trees) and Andacon (Evergreen Thunder) – with twenty men were to enter the colony by night and set fire to Lane's thatch. Lane, driven out by smoke and fumes and wearing only his night shirt, would be clubbed to death as soon as he appeared at his own door. Hariot was to receive the same treatment. The rest of the colonists would then be set upon by the overwhelming force of hired mercenaries. The night planned for the attack was 10 June, when the moon was new and there would be little light.

With knowledge of the details of the attack, Lane was able to devise ways of forestalling Pemisapan. He first sent word to the king that he was planning to go down to Croatoan to watch for the expected relief ships, then added '(although I in trueth had neither heard nor hoped for so good adventure)' and stated that he would like to take some Indians with him to help fish, and to buy some supplies for the four days they would be away. Pemisapan replied telling Lane that he would himself come over to Roanoke – but he delayed. He was unprepared for Lane's manoeuvre, and he speeded up the assembly of his mercenary army; the whole plan for attack was brought forward to 31 May – a night of full moon. The enemy, confused by being woken up from deep sleep, would be clear targets – a usual Indian tactic. Pemisapan procrastinated for eight days, giving his men time to assemble. Lane, aware of what was going on – for not all of Pemisapan's men were loyal to him – took the bull by the horns: 'that night I ment by the way to give them in the island a Camvisado.' What Lane is telling us is that he planned a night attack on the Indian village on the island, using a manoeuvre called a 'camisado' which meant simply that the attackers wore their shirts hanging out behind so as not to be fired on in the dark by their own side.

Just after sunset, as soon as it was dark, Lane sent a boat with Captain Vaughan over to the mainland to collect all the war canoes he could find. His orders were precise. Vaughan was to let pass any canoes going to the island, but to sink and kill the occupants of any going to the mainland. Thus Pemisapan on the mainland would know nothing of what was happening on Roanoke. Shortly, Vaughan met with two Indians in a canoe leaving the island, and his men beheaded them. Either because the English were seen in the light of the full moon, or because their victims cried out desperately for help, the look-outs on the island raised the alarm before Lane was ready to attack the village. The 'camisado' had misfired: most of the Indians fled into the woods, although Lane's own men managed to kill a few as they flitted through the moonlight.

That night Lane had little or no sleep. His men spent some time scouring the woods around the now deserted Indian village where not many months before they had been so generously entertained by Granganimeo's wife. As the embers of the village fire burnt down to ash, Lane made further plans. He could be certain that none of the Indians on the island had got through to Pemisapan on the mainland. Those who had fled were dispersed in the woods behind him, and Vaughan had dealt with the only canoe which had tried to cross the water. As far as Lane was concerned, he held the valuable asset of surprise; Pemisapan knew nothing of the night's work.

The next morning Lane set off for the mainland in the 'light horseman' and a canoe, with about twenty-seven men in all, leaving around forty men to defend the fort and to guard Skiko in case the Indians reassembled. Landing near the mainland village, Lane met one of Pemisapan's Indians and sent a message by him to the king saying that Lane was on his way to Croatoan, but had stopped off to complain about Osocan, one of Pemisapan's principal men, who, Lane cunningly claimed, had tried to set Skiko free in the night. If any flashes or noise of musket fire been noticed on the island by Pemisapan he would now assume that it was in connection with Osocan's attempt to free Skiko.

Lane's trick worked. The King, with seven or eight of his werowances around him, received Lane. This meeting would have taken place in the open area within the Indian village. Beyond the immediate circle of Lane and Pemisapan were some of the Roanoac warriors and beyond them were villagers going about their business. Close to him Lane had his bodyguard but his main party stayed back away from the central group, although within easy calling distance. This was one of Lane's courageous moments and he could not know how the encounter was going to turn out. Lane was facing a man who he knew was planning to kill him and slaughter his colonists, and he chose to meet him armed only with a sword, a pistol in his belt and accompanied by a few men. But he had the valuable advantage of surprise – Pemisapan was unaware that Lane knew of his plans.

As the Englishmen, protected by their helmets and corselets, alert for any treachery, walked towards Pemisapan, time must have stood still for Lane. Once close enough to the chief, Lane shouted out the watchword 'Christ our Victory' to his men beyond the tense circle, and Pemisapan was shot with a pistol fired by one of Lane's men. The Indian lay in the dust. In the inevitable confusion, Lane's men took Indian prisoners, being careful to spare 'Manteo's friends' – Croatoans friendly to the colonists and Manteo's own tribesmen. Pemisapan's body was forgotten.

But the king was not dead. Pemisapan, waiting until the confusion was absolute and seeing a way clear, leaped up as if he had never been shot and ran like a deer for the cover of the surrounding woods. After him went a small posse of colonists, letting off muskets and pistols at their flying target. A lucky shot from a petronel – a heavy cavalry pistol – aimed by Lane's Irish boy, shot the Indian through the buttock but didn't halt him. Edward Nugent, another Irishman, with an unnamed companion, the deputy provost, followed the king into the woods, an unwise move in view of the number of Indians sheltering there. But somehow the two overtook Pemisapan. To catch him they must have brought him down with another lucky shot for there was no way in which the English could match the Indian's running speed. Soon, the deputy provost and Nugent came out of the woods safely, spattered with blood but triumphant, Nugent carrying in his hands the grisly trophy of Pemisapan's head, still dripping blood.[1]

In this encounter we must award Lane full credit. If he had not struck first, Pemisapan would have killed him: the Governor of Virginia had carried the day. With the killing of Pemisapan, the attempt to annihilate the colonists was crushed and, as if to confirm the link with divinity, none of the colonists had been lost in the various encounters. A later Spanish report does suggest that four colonists were killed, and still other reports suggest that Lane indulged in ruthless reprisals against the Roanoacs, which would have been completely in his character.

What of the future at which Lane stared so bleakly? From his comments we gather he had clearly given up hope of an early arrival of relief ships from England. He had attempted to establish friendly relations with the local Indians and for a time had succeeded; he had avoided being drawn into any fighting in the purposeless Indian wars – the wars, in fact, seem to have been suspended whilst the tribes grappled with the common problem of the unwanted guests; he had carefully avoided the pitfall of dispossessing Indians from their own lands – a lesson no doubt learnt in Ireland; but his attempt to maintain friendly relations with his hosts, the Roanoacs, had been wrecked because the local tribes could not produce enough surplus food to support 100 colonists.

Had it succeeded, the attack by Pemisapan on the colony would have solved the Indians' problem. By defeating the Indians, Lane had removed immediate danger to the colonists, but had solved none of his long-term problems of survival. He had done all in his power. What was he to do next? Lane does not tell us. He leaves his account of events with Nugent emerging jubilant from the woods, making no mention of the Indians' reaction to their defeat, or to what immediately followed.

With this turbulent climax, however, the struggles of the new colony to survive òn England's farthest shore were all but over. Only eight days later there came a dramatic report from Stafford, still posted with his small party of men on Croatoan Island, thirty miles to the south: Sir Francis Drake had arrived with a relief fleet. His ships were sailing majestically up the Outer Banks, bringing the long awaited supplies.

11

'Ankered all without the Harbour'

Drake's West Indian voyage, which brought him back to England by way of Roanoke, was another of Walsingham's carefully calculated strikes at Spain's power, which spread across the Atlantic like the arms of an octopus. It was a subtle plan. The main aim of it was to intercept the *flotas* on their voyage home from Vera Cruz – now in modern Mexico, then the assembly point for bullion cargoes – so cutting off Spain's life-line. Without the treasure, previously mortgaged to the Genoa bankers, Philip's credit would be undermined; his armies in the Netherlands would go unpaid and lose their resolve; thus Spain would be brought to her knees without the wasteful extravagance of a campaign on land. It was a bold and intelligent plan. It also made a great deal of sense if, in the future, fleets similar to that of Drake could be maintained from a base on the American mainland – a base which hopefully was being established by Grenville and Lane.

On 14 September 1585, a fleet of twenty-six, under Admiral Sir Francis Drake, had left England. Sailing southward, the fleet let slip a *flota* carrying one of the greatest treasures ever brought to Spain. Drake only missed this glittering prize by the thinnest of margins – it arrive off Cadiz on 16 October! Brazenly putting into Vigo for fresh stores, Drake demanded the release of prisoners taken when Spain had impounded the English grain vessels in May earlier that same year. Delayed by storms, Drake's fleet could not sail for another six days, six days in which the English soldiers plundered and ransacked to little avail – the local population had removed all their treasures. Eventually, setting a course for the West Indies to make further inroads into Spain's empire, the fleet left, taking with them in triumph the ceremonial plate from Vigo cathedral.

Passing the Cape Verde Islands Drake paused at Santiago, but again the inhabitants had seen him coming and had taken to the hills with their valuables. Searching for treasure and frustrated in their endeavour, Drake's men took an Italian prisoner and a 'certain kind of torment was used to make him confess' where treasure was to be found.[1] From this unreliable informant all they were able to unearth was a cache of guns and powder.

To pass the time, the steward of the *Aid* was hanged for buggery with two of the ship's boys, but frustration turned to anger when one of the party, wandering away from the safety of his colleagues in search of the illusive booty, was beheaded by Spaniards who caught him, and 'ripping his belly took out his heart and carried them away, but let his body lie.'[2] In retaliation the English sacked and fired Santiago, finally leaving the island with the wind sending showers of sparks high into the air from the burning town, and a long trail of thick smoke straying far beyond the horizon, marking English displeasure at Spanish arrogance. Nothing more had been won than a few guns and sweetmeats. They also took with them a raging fever which struck the whole fleet within a few days, killing 300 men before it was spent: a sweet revenge from the Spanish point of view. At the hottest time of the year, cooped up in tiny ships, the wonder is that more did not die.

Pillaging and looting through the Caribbean, Drake took and briefly occupied first Santo Domingo then Cartagena, taking ships, cargoes, ransom money and any valuables he could find, and acquiring on the way some 1000 English, French and Dutch released from the galleys as well as 400 South American Indian, and black slaves. It had been the intention to occupy Cartagena and the Panama isthmus, and hold them while boat sections, carried in the ballast of the fleet, were assembled at Panama and launched as a Pacific fleet for further pillage of Spanish shipping. But the steaming swamps surrounding Cartagena caused havoc to the men's health, and although Drake's officers reluctantly voted to continue occupying the town, it was thought wiser to leave the place to the now hysterical Spaniards and the local Indians. Within a few days a Spanish rescue fleet arrived, but too late to catch the elusive Drake.

Making brief stops on uninhabited islands for water and meat, Drake and his fleet set course for San Agustín on the American mainland, the headquarters of Menéndez Marqués, who had

plenty of warning of the fleet's arrival. At a full assembly of
Captains, Drake had decided not to return directly to England,
in spite of the serious loss of men, but to seek out the Roanoke
colony. It will be remembered that the first news of the settlers
was brought to England by Captain John Arundell on 14 October
1585. As this was a month after Drake had sailed, Drake could
not have received the latest news of the colony's establishment,
and was relying on the original plan and on the colony's survival.
For the colony to have a better chance, the Spanish garrison at
San Agustín had to be exterminated.

Early in the morning of 27 May 1586 the fleet was off San
Agustín, and Drake landed at the head of his soldiers (see illustration). Marching a short way up a river bank (the river was too
shallow to take ships), he came upon a newly built fort on the other
side of the water. Further up river, to the south, was the unwalled
town of San Agustín. The access to the town was not easy; with
military cunning Menéndez Marqués had placed his fort at the top
of a fork in the river, a position which completely commanded any
attack from seaward. No matter which bank of the river the
invaders used, they would have to face cannon fire from the fort
and silence it before they could bring boats and men up to take the
town. The capture of the new fort was the key to the town. Cannons
were ferried ashore and dragged up the mile of river bank to a
position before the wooden walls of the fort. The first shot fired by
Christopher Carleill, Walsingham's stepson, brought down the
enemy's ensign – but this was only playing at attack.

At nightfall, Carleill had himself rowed over to see what sort of
problem the fort presented. The garrison within, thinking this to
be a major night assault, exchanged musket fire and, in panic, left
for the town. Carleill, not knowing the result of his nocturnal
prowling, returned to camp. Then, as the English settled down to
a night's rest with sentries posted, from the middle of the river
came the strange sound of a fife playing a tune familiar to those
who had fought in the Netherlands; it was 'William of Nassau',
William of Orange's song. As the sound came nearer, the alerted
and curious guard could see a Frenchman playing a fife and a
Dutchman rowing a boat. Both had been prisoners of the
Spaniards and they were bringing the good news that the fort was
deserted. The tune, of course, was a Protestant song and recognised
as friendly.

Next day the fort was occupied with no trouble by Carleill and twenty men, using a skiff and two pinnaces. The Spaniards, as the Frenchman had said, had gone, leaving behind them fourteen brass cannons and the garrison's wages – worth £2000 – in a chest. While Carleill and his men were in the fort their comrades on the other bank were assaulted from the cover of thick woods by Indians firing off arrows and making 'verie strawnge crie'.³ This unexpected attack was driven off with one fatal English casualty.

The official Spanish report of the taking of San Agustín paints a very different picture. No mention is made of the desertion of the fort – a deplorable piece of cowardice – but instead they make great play of the exaggerated size of the English forces, put at 12,000 men, with the Spanish valiantly fighting off many assaults.

> Behind certain sand dunes they drew up in formation, flags flying and drums beating; and . . . [we] . . . saw how the pinnaces and frigates and barges withdrew to the ships, and nineteen of them returned a second time and landed about four hundred men.
> With these troops they again attacked the fort, which met them with such fire from its artillery that they again withdrew with the loss of one pinnace which was sunk. It was publicly said that the men aboard were killed.⁴

Further determined attacks were driven off by the 'brave' Spaniards, but it was only in their imagination. The cornets, sackbuts and flageolets had perhaps played martial music – it was part of psychological warfare – but the roaring cannons, the sharp crack of musket fire, and the shouts of the attacking soldiery, existed only in the official reports. The fort had given in ignominiously.

The taking of the town followed easily the next day. It was a small settlement of about 250 houses, planned on the usual grid street lay-out, its only defence a few men. Apart from some desultory musket fire Drake's men were not hindered. Only one further fatal casualty was suffered: the Chief of Military Staff, Captain Powell, attempted to take a prisoner single-handed for questioning and was killed by a Spanish horseman and two foot soldiers. Drake's men had the town to themselves and taking what had been left in the way of furniture – including even locks and bolts from the doors for the use of the colonists on Roanoke – they set fire to the town and the crops in the surrounding fields before retiring to the fort to rest for three days. Inside the town's fort they found the treasure-chest containing the 6000 ducats and close by the fort a small caravel with more treasure and a terrified child who had been left behind in the scramble to leave. (The treasure was taken, but the child returned to the Spaniards.) The stores of food which Drake had hoped to find had been taken out of the town before the attack.

Some six days after they had arrived, Drake and his party left, having meanwhile careened one of their ships on the beach. Before they departed they destroyed the fort, leaving the Spaniards to return from the cover of the forest to pick over the ashes of their possessions. Once the outlying fort had fallen, there was little Menéndez Marqués could have done. He had only eighty men, a great many non-combatants, and was surrounded by hostile Indians. Nevertheless, he had received a nasty fright, which was now compounded by three negro slaves, who escaped from Drake's men in the confusion of taking the town. They told of the Englishmen's intention of attacking Santa Elena further to the north. It was also correctly guessed that the slaves – particularly the slaves, for no one in England kept slaves – and the door furniture were taken for the benefit of English colonists, based in Florida perhaps. But Drake's victory was not substantial: no shattering blow had been struck and San Agustín was soon rebuilt and re-garrisoned.

Drake and his fleet now set course to attack Santa Elena, as the escaped slaves had warned. The entrance to the town was a difficult one with shoals and bars unknown to Drake's navigator. Prudence prevailed and Drake had to be content to anchor the fleet a few miles north to take on water, fuel and a mast for one of his vessels. Leaving Santa Elena the fleet held its course for Lane's settlement.

Approximately seven days after leaving San Agustín, on the 8 or 9 June 1586, the fleet was sailing slowly north off the Outer Banks, keeping a sharp watch for signals from the low, forested shoreline. Here too were dangerous shoals and banks which kept them three to six miles from land, but they had already been sighted by Captain Stafford on Croatoan Island, near Cape Hatteras, who feared that this might be a Spanish fleet looking for the settlers. So far from the shore the ships would have been very difficult to distinguish: from a height of thirty feet the horizon is just over six miles distant, and the June heat haze would have distorted the outline of the vessels making detail uncertain.

The arrival of twenty-three sail was reported to Lane on Roanoke and the answer to be cautious sent back to Stafford. If Lane's account is to be believed this was an astonishing feat of communication. Croatoan to Roanoke and back is a round trip of 100 miles and Stafford had Lane's answer within a day! At last Stafford was satisfied that the fleet was friendly, and lit 'one speciall great fire'. The banks are now bare of trees, but they were often ablaze with forest fires, either caused spontaneously in the hot, dry summer or by Indians, burning off areas for new planting of maize. But Stafford's signal was recognised and the fleet stopped its slow and stately course, heaved to, and a skiff was sent to the distant shoreline. Nothing is said in contemporary accounts of the undoubted excitement of this meeting on the lonely, alien shore; nor of Stafford's men running into the surf to help pull the skiff onto the beach with shouts of welcome. Infuriatingly, this moment is passed over with only the briefest of statements: that the skiff took on one of the colonists to guide the fleet into Port Ferdinando.

If this is correct then it was Stafford who sailed north along the coast to pilot Drake's fleet, for it was he who carried a letter from Drake to Lane, written when the ships were off the entrance to the Sound and Roanoke: 'we ankered all without the harbour in a wild road at sea about two miles from the shore'. The sea would have been running an uneasy swell, for unknown to the English a remarkably severe succession of hurricanes was about to hit them. Drake had expected to find Grenville and his ships still with Lane, and it must have been some disappointment to find that, far from there being a safe harbour and a small fleet, there was only a band of colonists living primitively and offering a very exposed anchorage offshore. Stafford arrived at Lane's headquarters on Roanoke Island after a walk of twenty miles, suggesting that he may have been landed on Bodie Island. Drake was offering help – supplies of clothing and food. The offer of food was generous in view of the fact that he was already running short himself, but Drake had plenty of clothing which Lane's party lacked. He also made available, should the colonists need them, munitions, boats, barks and pinnaces, as well as negro slaves from the Spanish galleys and the released South American Indians for use as labour. Drake had not seen for himself the conditions on the island; the arrival of 300 liberated slaves would have thrown into total disarray the local subsistence economy.

The following day, 10 June 1586, Lane visited Drake aboard his flagship, *Elizabeth Bonaventure*, taking with him the officers of the colony who effectively made up the council. There in the great cabin Drake, with the consent of his officers, offered Lane a more realistic choice: either Lane could have one of the fleet's ships, a pinnace, and certain boats, with sufficient crews to man them and victuals enough to supply 100 men for four months, so that he could finish charting the area before returning to England; or, if the explorations had already been completed to Lane's satisfaction, Drake offered to take the colonists – now numbering 103 – back with him to England. Lane and his council gratefully accepted the first of the alternatives.

Immediately the decision had been made, arrangements went ahead, and by the day after the meeting the *Francis* of 70 tons, a fast bark, had been received in charge by Lane's men and stores were being stowed aboard. Also handed over were two pinnaces and four boats, and crew to man the various vessels. On 13 June, the hurricane struck. The whirlwind tempest was moving north and, roughly following the coastline, it caught them all unawares. For three or four days the wind blew with force from every direction, the seas became peaks of livid, tumultuous foam, and the waves dashed themselves onto the shore. Boats and pinnaces were caught up and smashed onto the beach in the thunderous roar of breaking surf. Lightning of terrifying clarity cracked around the ships, illuminating the shore and the far horizon in brief brilliant flashes, while thunder exploded overhead like the noise of gods in a tormented frenzy. Hailstones fell 'as Bigge as hennes egges', threatening to smash the head of anyone caught in the open. Waterspouts appeared out of the murky blackness sweeping up boats and pinnaces in their path, carrying the debris up into the black clouds glowering above. The hurricane struck so suddenly that Drake had no time to run for the comparative safety of the open sea to weather the storm. The ferocity of the wind and the strength of the waves broke cables and fractured anchors. The unusually long duration of the storm suggested a succession of two or more hurricanes with electric storms and other atmospheric disturbances sandwiched between them. Ashore, matters can only have been slightly better than at sea. It was a terrifying and chastening experience for all, even those used to the ways of tropical weather. None dared to guess what it might portend. By the time the violence had subsided some of the fleet had vanished, among them the *Francis* with all those on board.

12

'A Wild Fire Arrow'

When Drake reassembled his scattered ships, the fleet had been reduced by four vessels, including the *Francis* with the stores for the colony on board, and some of Lane's men. But the *Francis* had not, in fact, been lost. Lane's men aboard her had had enough of Virginia, and they used the excuse of the storm to sail for England. They arrived home before Drake.

Drake made a second generous offer of help, now that only the *Bark Bonner* could be spared. She was not an ideal vessel for the job. At 170 tons her draught was too deep to clear the sand bars into the Sound and Drake specified that she would have to remain in the sea-way. With the ship Drake offered crew to sail her and sufficient provisions to supply the colonists on the voyage home. He was proposing that Lane should complete his charting in his own time and then sail home in the *Bark Bonner*. At the same time Drake asked Lane for a list of requirements to support the colony until they planned to leave Virginia. Alternatively, Drake offered to take them all back to England with him, thus abandoning the settlement.

Lane called together what remained of his council to consider the new offers. He and his officers were of the opinion that Grenville's relief ships would not arrive. (In that they were wrong; one was a bare two weeks away, and Grenville himself with eight vessels was not far behind.) The recent tempest had plainly shaken their resolve. The storm was 'God's wrath and punishment for the outrages committed against the Indians', clear indication that Lane had taken savage revenge. They saw Drake's offer to take them home with him as 'the very hand of God'.

As soon as the decision was taken, the colonists began packing the few things they had to take with them. Drake's sailors were anxious to be away from the dangerous Virginia coast and to claim their share of the prize money in England. The sea was still rough and, in the near panic to be off, many of Lane's – much to his distress – and Hariot's writings were lost, as well as some of White's drawings, and a collection of pearls.

No doubt the seamen considered the pearls and papers as rubbish and unnecessary baggage. From our point of view the lost writings of Lane and Hariot were the most valuable part of the colonists' baggage. In Lane's words they 'were by the Saylors cast overboard'. We can sympathise with his agony. The rush to be away was so frantic that three of Drake's men, who had been sent up-country returning Skiko to his father, Menatonon, were left behind! No mention is made of what became of the passengers Drake had acquired on the way, the slaves released from the Caribbean galleys and brought to Roanoke to serve the colonists. Approximately 100 Turks probably returned to England and were repatriated, and there is a strong possibility that the 100 black and 300 Indian ex-slaves were cast ashore on Roanoke. Manteo, at least, returned to England with the colonists and appears to have become so Europeanised that he wore Elizabethan dress and preferred life with his English friends to the primitive existence he had known with his tribe on Croatoan Island. Within two or three days of Drake making his offer, the fleet, with Lane and the remaining colonists safely aboard, weighed anchor. After giving sincere thanks to God, the English were off on a course set for Newfoundland, where they would take in water and fish on the way back to Portsmouth. They arrived home at the end of July.

Before the end of June, the first relief ship arrived off Port Ferdinando. Its occupants spent some time looking for the colonists, but when it was obvious that they were not to be found, the unnamed vessel returned, with its stores, to England. The venture, financed out of Ralegh's pocket, was a loss. Grenville next arrived with eight ships and a full year's supply of stores, but two months or more too late. His arrival, so anxiously awaited by Lane since early April, had been delayed by his trying unsuccessfully to intimidate the inhabitants of Madeira into supplying his fleet with water. It would have been impossible for Grenville to have arrived as early as Lane had hoped; to have done so would have meant leaving in February, traditionally no month to sail due to fierce winter storms in the Bay and Atlantic. Grenville had tried to get away in mid-April but was delayed until the first days of May. He had resisted the temptation to pillage and plunder the Caribbean, as he had done the year before, but had held his course for Florida after leaving Madeira. He probably arrived off Virginia in mid-August 1586.

At the deserted settlement and fort Grenville and his men found the body of one colonist – perhaps one of the three left behind – and the body of an Indian swinging from a tree. Standing in the empty site, with the evidence all around him of the colonists' hurried departure, Grenville faced considerable disappointment. Beyond the line of the Outer Banks the masts of his ships could just be seen at anchor, while the distant noise of the surf mingled with the ceaseless rustling of the nearby woods. The grisly tableau of the two bodies posed a sinister riddle. Why had his colonists gone, leaving no word of their plans? Were the struggle to collect costly supplies, the harassing delays in leaving England, the deliberate policy to avoid privateering in the Caribbean to arrive as early as possible all in vain? Grenville cast around the area for clues. The Roanoac Indians, decimated and frightened by Lane's recent reprisals, had moved off the island to Dasemunkepeuc. The Indian village on the island was deserted and as desolate as the fort and settlement; there was no answer to be found there either. Grenville's men at last managed to catch three Indians, but they were slippery prisoners and two escaped back into the woods. From the remaining, terrified Indian Grenville at last learned of Drake's arrival, the frightening hurricane, and the colonists' hurried departure from Virginia. Wisely the prisoner said nothing of events preceding Lane's going. This news was not as bad as Grenville had feared, but it meant the end of the first colony.

Although Grenville had with him a year's supply of food and a total of 400 men, of which a little under a third would have been soldiers useful only in combat, he did not re-establish the colony on the scale of that which he had left in 1585. He was, however, 'unwilling to loose the possession of the Countrie, which the Englishmen had so long held'. Compromising, a bad thing in this instance, he left fifteen men under the leadership of Masters Coffin and Chapman, together with four cannons and supplies for two years. Although some of the new colonists may have sailed with

Grenville to Roanoke the year before, and so had some
experience of the place, the majority of them had no practical
knowledge of how to survive in a strange land – and they had no
idea of the recent difficulties with the local Indians. Nevertheless
the emotions of these very brave, or very stupid men, as Grenville
sailed from Port Ferdinando, disappearing hull down over the
horizon, are not difficult to imagine. They were left alone on an
alien shore with the recently dug grave of the dead Englishman,
the unsolved mystery of the dead Indian, their two years' supply
of food stacked into the storehouse, and four cast-iron cannons for
defence. Imagination on their part would have been a
disadvantage.

Sailing with Grenville went the unfortunate Indian. His fate is
uncertain, but in the Bideford parish register for 1588 under
baptisms is the entry for an adult christening: 'Raleigh, a
Wynganditoian . . . 27 March'. Whether or not this Indian living
in Grenville's household is he, is open to speculation. At all events
this unfortunate Christian was destined never to see 'Wingan de
Coy' again; he died and was buried in Bideford churchyard on
7 April 1589, just over twelve months after he was baptised.

By leaving Virginia in the third week of August, – the same
time as the previous year – Grenville may have hoped to repeat
his profitable luck. He certainly followed the same course,
running to the Azores until, with many men sick and thirty-four
dead, perhaps from scurvy, he turned about and sailed 1500
miles to Newfoundland for fresh food and water. Then he
returned to the Azores to cruise through the islands in the hope of
taking a prize. He was not particularly successful: he missed the
flota by weeks. After five months at sea he had not sighted a single
enemy sail! To keep up his men's morale, Grenville wasted time
taking a small vessel sailing between the islands with passengers
aboard not worth a ransom; most of those taken died. On an
island off San Miguel Grenville came upon a ship careened
helplessly on the beach with her cargo of half-cured stinking
hides piled up above high water on the foreshore and the crew in
disarray. This too was an unsatisfactory prize. The English took
the hides but generously left the ship for the crew to finish work
on. They had a modicum of luck, shared with an English frigate,
when together, they took a Spaniard from Puerto Rico. This was
obviously one of those voyages which would never go well; there

was nothing for it but to return to England. With the colonists gone from Virginia it had been a pointless journey, but they had at least, returned with most of the colonists' supplies intact. Grenville arrived back in England the day after Christmas, 1586.

For the small group left on Roanoke Island, Christmas came not at all. Left with no particular task except to be a presence, the colonists passed their time in almost total idleness, since their food was assured for two years. Some time in the early autumn, the surviving Roanoac Indians made up their minds to be rid of their last unwelcome guests. They could have concluded with perfect logic that their aggression had paid off: the main party of foreigners had gone, and there were not enough of the new arrivals to pose much of a threat. The Roanoacs' strength had been broken and, perhaps because of their reduced numbers, they called on the Secotan tribe – a tribe once their enemy – for help.

Thirty warriors hid themselves in the darkness of the woods near the English settlement, where the caretaker colonists were carelessly living in the houses and not, as would have been wiser, within the fort. They had been lulled into a false sense of security. The Indians watching from amongst the trees counted eleven Englishmen. They did not feel outnumbered. And, with cunning, two of the Indians showed themselves by walking into the wide open area cleared of trees before the settlement. The colonists called to their unexpected visitors and by signals indicated that two of their senior members would come unarmed to talk with the pair. Dulled by weeks of inactivity they omitted to cover their two colleagues with loaded muskets. The four approached one another. One Indian was welcoming the leading Englishman when treachery came: the other Indian drew a wooden sword from under his mantle and struck the colonist from behind.

The hidden Indians broke cover, no doubt with war-cries echoing over the roofs of the settlement and in the woods behind. The remaining colonist ran back to his companions, who took shelter in one of the houses. There they prepared for a siege. Around the house surged the thirty Indian warriors, grotesque in warpaint, and giving blood-chilling war-cries. It is likely that the Englishmen were so unprepared that they were cut off from their firearms stored in the fort; they had only a bow with them. The Indians used the tactic they had planned earlier: they set fire to the thatch, driving out the colonists with the smoke. The English ran out 'amongst the Savages, with whome they skirmished above an howre'. This seems overlong for a skirmish with a small party of colonists outnumbered three to one, and it is remarkable that only one of the colonists was killed. He was 'shotte into the mouthe with an arrow whereof he died'. One Indian succumbed to a direct hit in the side by a 'wild fire arrow'. Firearms were quite obviously not used by the besieged; the 'wild fire arrow' which caught one Indian was probably a missile returned by the colonists which had already been discharged by the Indians to fire the thatch of the houses. The cannons, had they been to hand, would have been quite useless.

Eventually the surviving colonists made a break. Running for their boat on the beach nearby, they clambered in and rowed away as fast as they could for Hatarask, stopping only to collect four comarades who had been oyster fishing up one of the many creeks. Apart from the two colonists killed, others had been wounded in the skirmishing around the settlement. It was more than they had expected for their two years' easy life on Roanoke Island and they never returned to the colony. They remained on Hatarask for a time 'but afterwards departed whither, as yet we know not'. They were never heard of again and Roanoke was abandoned to the Indians for a second time.

Resulting from Ralegh's first colony in Virginia under Governor Lane there were, by the end of 1586, at least sixteen Englishmen at large on the mainland of America who have never been accounted for: the three who were marooned when Lane left in such a hurry, and thirteen of the fifteen put ashore by Grenville. In addition there were, very likely, 400 liberated black and Indian slaves existing in the same area.

Ralegh's first venture in colonising Virginia had brought mixed results. He had done well enough financially, thanks to the privateering aspect of the voyages, and the investors could count their speculation a success, although not a spectacular one. Ralegh must have been frustrated that the Queen had not allowed him to take an active part. Had he been allowed to go, this story would have been entirely different: America would have made a splendid theatre for one who liked the public eye. Instead, Lane had steered the colony through privations and dangers and had achieved the remarkable result of losing only four colonists from sickness – and they were said to have been 'feeble weake and sickly persons before they ever came thither'. Pedro Diaz, the pilot of the *Santa Maria*, taken off Bermuda in 1585 – he was unwillingly caught up in colonising until he escaped by jumping into the sea off the Cape Verde Islands in 1588 – said that four colonists were killed by Indians. This is not quite what Lane would have us believe! It was undoubtedly an achievement for Lane that out of 108 colonists he lost only at most eleven, particularly when it is remembered that they were living off unusual diets. Furthermore Lane had proved that it was possible for a settlement to survive through the winter, given the goodwill of the Indians.

Thomas Hariot provided the first and most valuable account of Indian habits and the natural life and geology of the area, supported by John White's water colours. We can only regret the writings lost by Drake's sailors. A survey had been carried out, sufficiently detailed to provide a working chart, and, although no useful minerals had been found by the German miners, both Lane and Hariot were confident that copper and perhaps gold would be discovered. Pearls had been found in Chesapeake. They were also confident that a colony in Virginia could be self-supporting, and would in time make a contribution to England's wealth. Just what might be exported from the colony, neither man could say with certainty but they both mentioned minerals and the types of timber to be exploited, as well as crops which might be developed. They missed what became the main support of the Virginian colony – tobacco – although Hariot describes how the crop was grown and smoked by the Indians.[1] There was disappointment about the lack of a safe anchorage, but the keen hope was that Chesapeake would be found more than adequate. All in all, prospects looked good even if Virginia did not promise vast riches such as Spain had tapped in South America. It was worth making another attempt.

PART TWO

The Second Colony

13

'The Fort Raised Down'

As soon as Sir Richard Grenville arrived back in England with his eight ships in December 1586, he took himself to London to begin organising, with John White, an expedition to take a second colony to Virginia, based on the sound experience gained from the first. But this was interrupted when he returned to his home in Bideford, in February 1587. There he was occupied in fitting out three ships, which included Ralegh's *Roebuck,* for a privateering venture, acting under letters of reprisal against Spain granted by the Queen for losses suffered. It is very likely that he planned to take about fifty colonists from the West County to support the fifteen he imagined were still holding out in Roanoke. But in the event the three ships never sailed, for Grenville was diverted into overseeing the defences in the West against an expected invasion by Spain.[1]

Meanwhile, in London, John White was left with the main work of organising the second colony. This was to be altogether different in concept. Lane's colony of 108 men had been a military establishment, a paid garrison with no interest in self-sufficiency from the land. Although this policy had the advantage of taking no agricultural land from the Indians it did rely on their goodwill in providing food. Clearly this had not worked. The second colony was to be an established community of families, volunteer investors, each allocated 500 acres from which they had to become self-supporting. The plan allowed for between 150 and 200 colonists – in fact only 110 were finally settled – under the first Governor, John White, and twelve Assistants of the 'Cittie of Ralegh in Virginia'. The new 'Cittie of Ralegh' was to be sited in Chesapeake. On 7 January 1587 the 'Cittie' received from William Dethick, Garter King of Arms, its grant of arms, a simple red cross quartering a gold field and in the top left corner a roebuck – Ralegh's crest. At the same time an impressive coat of arms was cooked up for John White of London, gentleman; it tells us nothing about his family or where he came from. The twelve Assistants likewise had arms designed for them. Almost immediately an appeal was made for investor-colonists. From the names of the eventual 110 who finally sailed, it is impossible to assign origins or personal histories; they were single people, male and female, and family groups, possibly some with servants, who had capital enough to invest in the venture. It is not clear what attracted them to the idea of the colony, or why they should have entrusted themselves to what could be nothing but a hazardous adventure. To be sure, the advertisements for the project gave only the advantages, but there were rumours emanating from the colonists who had returned that all had not been quite as told.

While Grenville was occupied in the defence of the West Country, John White in London was not so distracted. Some of the settlers had gathered in London and by late March, White, with Fernandez once again (with whom he would shortly be at loggerheads), was ready to sail to the West Country picking up more settlers on the way. There was the *Lion* of 120 tons, with White as Captain and Fernandez as Master (perhaps the vessel of the same name in the 1585 expedition); a fly-boat, unnamed, whose Master was Edward Spicer; and a pinnace, likewise unnamed, under Captain Edward Stafford. They all sailed round the coast to Portsmouth where fitting out was completed and perhaps more settlers joined the ships. On 26 April 1587 the three vessels crossed the Solent, arriving the same day at Cowes in the Isle of Wight, where they remained eight days before returning to Portsmouth. During this period John White was in touch with Sir George Carey at Carisbrooke Castle, six miles from Cowes. It is very likely that Carey had been an investor in the 1585 venture; he was vice-admiral of Hampshire, and self-styled 'Governor' of the Isle of Wight and, like so many whose estates were on the Channel coast, Carey was involved in privateering. What was arranged between the two is not completely clear, but Carey too had letters of reprisal for the operation of three privateers under Captain William Irish. Irish, in Carey's pay, sailed for the West Indies ahead of White, perhaps with more colonists but more likely with supplies for the colony. His intention was, seemingly, to use the Chesapeake harbour and the new colony as a privateering base. From Portsmouth, White sailed down Channel to Plymouth, arriving there on 6 May. The last stores, fresh water and perhaps some West Country colonists were put on board the three vessels.

White's narrative of the voyage has this simple entry for 8 May 1587: 'we waied anker at Plymouth, and departed thence for Virginia'. This statement does not do justice to what must have been a dramatic and emotional scene played out on the dockside at Plymouth as the first English colonists actually to have bought a stake in Virginia, to have committed their money and their persons to their belief in a prosperous future, said goodbye to their relatives and their country for the last time. But then White had a curt way of expressing himself. The party was sailing two years and one month after Grenville had set out from Plymouth with the first colony; this time, at least the settlers knew something of the country they were bound for under their new Governor.

John White is yet another shadowy figure. One of the difficulties in research is that his was a common name. A John White was Mayor of Plymouth in 1583–4; another was a prominent figure in the Portsmouth area. Yet again there were Whites in Ireland, tenants of the Butlers, Earls of Ormond, and the Butler arms on John's escutcheon may indicate an Irish connection. There was John White, a fishmonger of London, who was Captain of the 40 ton *Balinus* in 1591, with letters of reprisal against Spain. It has even been suggested that the relatively humble John White who made the drawings of 1585–6 was not the same man as the important Governor of the 'Cittie of Ralegh' in 1587. This argument holds no water. White tells us that he had been on all five voyages to Virginia and there is no evidence of any other John White being involved in the ventures. We must fall back on the scant details he gives us of himself.

He was a skilled surveyor and draughtsman, indicating an education of some specialisation. One would normally expect to find this type of man employed in the greater households, surveying, drawing and illustrating maps of estates. As with his name, the position of surveyor was not uncommon; perhaps his maps lie anonymously in the muniment room of some English country house never to be acknowledged. The last we hear of him is in 1593, when he wrote to Richard Hakluyt from Kilmore,

County Cork. Over a hundred years later, Sir Hans Sloane was in touch with White's descendants and, after 1709, acquired a volume of John White's drawings bearing the inscription to 'my soon Whit' on 11 April 1673, which only tells us that he had relatives who survived him. For one who played such a large part in colonising Virginia, the canvas is almost blank. He did, however, have a daughter Elenor, the wife of Ananias Dare, and they both went with him to Virginia in 1587.

Of White's son-in-law, Ananias Dare, a little can be said. In 1594 letters of administration were granted to his nearest relative, Robert Satchfield, for the care of his estate. For by then he was assumed to be dead by church law. His residence had been in the parish of St Bride, Fleet Street, London.[2] The matter had been raised because his illegitimate son John was making a claim to his father's estate.

The next entry in White's journal is also disappointing in its curtness, but it represents the first of his complaints against Fernandez – and after only eight days at sea. 'The 16 [May] Simon Ferdinando Master of our Admirall, lewdly forsooke our Flie boate leaving her distressed in the Baye of Portingall.' The smaller boat had run into trouble in a storm, and Fernandez, delayed by a late start, was anxious to make the Caribbean in the shortest possible time, to engage in his favourite and profitable sport of privateering against the Spanish. One can see Fernandez, when confronted by John White, shrugging the matter off as being of no consequence, allowing the 100 ton fly-boat either to look after itself or be lost. It was no concern of his that the vessel carried White's colonists, whose skills would be needed in Virginia; the colonists were a damn nuisance and cluttered up his ships when he wanted to clear decks for action against the Spanish. Fernandez made it increasingly clear that he had no time for these landlubber settlers who had no experience of seafaring. White acquiesced, when a stronger man would have stood up to Fernandez. White was the Governor of the colony but Fernandez had complete jurisdiction over the seafaring side. Furthermore he was one of the Assistants appointed in January to govern the colony; he too had been given arms with the style of gentleman, of London. Fernandez was notoriously difficult, and plainly White could not manage him.

The voyage across the Atlantic is not mentioned, so very

commonplace had it become. Following the coast of Portugal and North Africa to avoid the westerlies, White's vessels took a west-south-west course from the Canaries to catch the north-east trade winds which would blow the ships across 3500 miles of empty Atlantic Ocean. Forty-two days after leaving Portsmouth, they sighted Dominica. This was a much slower passage than that of twenty-eight days made in 1585. The ships were averaging barely 120 miles each day. Fernandez could have calculated the day's speed by estimating the time taken for a piece of flotsam to pass the length of the ship or, perhaps, by log-line, which was then a new navigational instrument. The log-line consisted of a small piece of board attached to the end of a long thin line. The board, when dropped over the stern, would cause the line to run out and, from the moment the board was in the water, a seaman would begin timing one minute as accurately as possible. There were sand-glasses for the purpose but more often some verse lasting approximately one minute would be recited, or someone would count up to 120. When the minute had elapsed the line would be stopped and the amount of line run out measured. By means of a simple sum the speed of the ship could be calculated. This method only provided a rough estimate, for it measured distance through the water and not over the ground. Running against a current would give a more optimistic reading than running with it: both measurements were inaccurate anyway.

This haphazard system was the only way of calculating longitude, or distance east and west. The latitude, or distance north or south of the equator was more accurately calculated by means of the backstaff, used to measure the height of a heavenly body above the horizon. The sun at midday provided the easiest and most accurate 'shot'. Again, use of so primitive an instrument introduced errors; horizon and sun had to be caught at the precise moment when the vessel was riding the top of a wave. Thomas Hariot, observing these difficulties, experimented with an improved backstaff and recommended that three sightings should be taken for greater accuracy. Even so, there would be differences due to personal idiosyncrasy – the position of the eye in the head and the contour of the cheek. When taking a shot of the sun by means of the backstaff, the dazzling light added to the problems. Navigation was composed of estimates and errors, tested by inaccurate instruments, and the whole multiplied by the time spent out of sight of land. Ultimately it was corrected only by the navigator's experience – there was no other way.

Forty-two days on the run must have meant that some time was spent becalmed. As the tropical sun beat down from a copper sky, the heat on board was insufferable, with no breeze to cool the air trapped between decks, where every gun-port gaped open. The oak deck planks became too hot to touch even with tough bare feet, and the heat penetrated to the cabins beneath. Overhead, the sails hung like sad flags, limp bleached and sparkling with sea salt crystals. Tempers frayed, and White nurtured his hatred of Fernandez. All on board prayed for a wind to move them from the furnace in which they were trapped.

The breeze came, tugging diffidently at first at the limp canvas, then freshening to a wind. The sails cracked out, and bellied taut, pulling the ship forward; at the mast head the streamer jauntily pointed towards America. The stem of the ship began moving through the water with its lion figurehead resolutely leading the way.

In the warm nights, the watch could hear the heavy breathing of a nearby porpoise, or the sigh of a whale as it blew. These were both very human–sounding noises, encouraging the belief in mermaids. By day dolphins raced the ship, chasing fish. Up to two days from the Caribbean, land birds were sighted, a far more accurate indication of position than navigation. Then there was the smell of land long before it was sighted, warm and green like a hot-house of growing things. The *Lion* made Dominica on 19 June 1587. Fernandez' calculations, estimates, guesses and experience had brought them to the entrance of the Caribbean and, although he did not know it, the fly-boat was only two days behind.

The following three weeks were spent in cruising through the islands. White attempted to get Fernandez to call at Hispaniola to buy cattle and other stores for the colony, while Fernandez procrastinated in the hope of picking up a prize. In the event neither was satisfied, and White expressed his frustration in his journal. His criticisms of Fernandez were often justified, but now the two were so out of harmony that White blamed the Portuguese for every misfortune.

Passing to the north of Dominica, Fernandez had followed the usual north-west course for Hispaniola, coming to anchor three days later off Santa Cruz Island (now St Croix in the U S Virgin Islands). Santa Cruz was said by Fernandez to be uninhabited; it was simply hair-splitting on White's part to note the discovery of huts and eleven Caribs. Here the colonists were set ashore for three days and nights while the ships were cleaned and aired. The visitors built temporary cabins for themselves above high water on the beach and took in their first impressions of a foreign, tropical land. Their stay was not altogether successful and the colonists suffered from inexperience. The only water was from a brackish and clearly infected pool; many who drank it became ill, and others who washed in it experienced burning and swelling which closed their eyes for up to six days. Still others experimented with eating 'a small fruite, like greene apples'. These were the poisonous type of pome and the effect was 'a sudden burning in their mouthes, and swelling of their tongues so bigge that some of them could not speak'. The poison, although not lethal, was very unpleasant and its effects lasted for twenty-four hours. One of the smallest children suffered its effects through his mother's milk; the mother must have been either Elizabeth Viccars or Joyce Archard, the only two women with children. Hakluyt, in publishing White's narrative, noted in the margin, 'Circumspection to be used in strange places'. On that first night the men caught five sea turtles, some so large that sixteen men could barely carry them from the water's edge. This was useful fresh meat to supplement the often inedible ship's diet they had endured.

The following days were spent in searching the island for potable water. Some was found too far off to supply the ships, and too late for those who had tasted the pond water. The pinnace under Captain Stafford was sent off to Vieques Island towards Puerto Rico to take on sheep which Fernandez said would be found there. White took great pleasure in assuring us that 'our Simon' was wrong; there were no sheep on Vieques. After three days the colonists, recovering from their swellings and irritations, returned aboard and the two vessels left for St John's Island, meeting up with the empty-handed pinnace and Captain Stafford on the way. It was on St John's that Grenville had established a large fort in Mosquetal Bay and built a new pinnace whilst waiting for his scattered fleet to arrive in 1585. It was to

Mosquetal Bay that Fernandez came, for he knew he would find there a supply of fresh drinking water to refill his casks. This was a legitimate stop, yet White made the acid comment, 'we spent three daies unprofitably in taking in freshe water, spending in the meantime more beer, than the quantity of the water came to'. White would have been even more critical had Fernandez allowed the ships to run out of water. Two of the Irish members of White's colony, David Glavin and Dennis Carrol, deserted ship at Mosquetal Bay. Glavin was captured by the Spanish and spent some years in the galleys. Referring to his desertion Glavin said 'he was told to make his escape which he did'. That Glavin should choose the certainty of being taken by the Spanish rather than continue with the main party of colonists is strange, particularly since Glavin's wife, Elizabeth, was also a colonist and remained! Carrol was never heard of again and his choice is not so inexplicable: he had no ties to keep him.

Another difference between White and Fernandez arose over salt, an essential supply for the colony. Remembering how Lane had been sent for salt in Puerto Rico, White organised a boat party to land at Rojo Bay, St John's, taking with him a heavy guard comprising thirty muskets and ten pikemen with shields. Fernandez had previously set the colonists to making sacks for the salt; now he changed his mind. With a display of extrovert theatricals, which did not deceive White, Fernandez told him that he did not know if salt could be found at Rojo Bay at all, and that if they went and bad weather blew up, the *Lion* would have to run for the open sea leaving them behind. White tells an unconvincing tale of how, as Fernandez was talking to him, 'he caused the lead to be cast, and having craftily brought the ship in three fathoms, and a halfe water, he suddenly began to sweare, and teare God in peeces, dissembling great danger, crying to him at the helme, beare up hard, beare up hard; so we went off, and were disappointed of our salt by his means'. White cannot be telling the whole story. For the helm to respond, the vessel would have been under way; and White must have heard the anchor being raised by the watch because it was a noisy operation. What is more likely is that White, hearing the anchor being raised, rushed out on deck to remonstrate with Fernandez, who would have had some sail set and a man at the helm. No doubt White took the pilot's mind off the immediate problem and he only came back to it at the leadsman's cry – the automatic reaction of any pilot. Then Fernandez cutting short the exchange, let fly a string of epithets in his broken English, calling to the helmsman to 'Bear-up hard! Bear-up hard!' to bring the ship round into deeper water. However it happened White had been outmanoeuvred again.

No doubt that night White nurtured his antagonism for Fernandez as he wrote up his journal in his cabin. The next day, as they passed down St John's Island with the coast to starboard, he made another attempt to get his own way. White was not being at all subtle because as long as he was on the *Lion* Fernandez was in charge. Fernandez never actually disagreed with the Governor or argued with him; he simply outflanked, or ignored him. It can have done White's authority with his colonists no good, and no doubt they were as distressed as he to see their leader outwitted in these undignified wrangles.

As they passed down the coast White asked to put into Boqueron Bay to collect young plants: oranges, pineapples and bananas, for the colony. He had seen them there in 1585 and even sketched them. 'Our Simon' would have none of this, and denied there were any such fruit trees growing there. White called on some of the colonists who had been with him in 1585 – John Wright and James Lacy are the only two colonists listed in both ventures – to confirm that there were fruit trees in the Bay. As a compromise Fernandez offered to put into Isabela on Hispaniola for White to buy cattle and provisions from Alanson, Fernandez' French friend and merchant on the island who had assisted them in 1585. With that White had to be content.

On 4 July they sighted the coast of Hispaniola, and White prepared himself for the snub which he knew must come. 'But that day passed and we saw no preparation for landing on Hispaniola,' White lamely tells us. At last on the following day he could keep quiet no longer. White, by making enquiries, had discovered what he suspected: they had sailed right by Isabela with no word said. Filled with frustration and indignation, White reminded the pilot of his promise. Fernandez had, of course, been expecting this confrontation, possibly even looking forward to it. Alanson, he explained, had been transported to Spain after the events of 1585, Ralegh had told him as much and he had it from the Ambassador. There was no point in putting into Isabela, or anywhere else for stores. Governor White could do no more than choke back his anger and rage.

Holding the same north-westerly course Fernandez left Hispaniola astern and, passing through Silver Bank, anchored of East Caicos Island where he said the colonists would find two salt ponds. White, unable to get the better of Fernandez, kept his own council and reported in his narrative with pleasure that no salt was found. However, it did give the colonists the chance to take some recreation ashore: some went wildfowling, others successfully hunted swans, while some searched for the elusive salt ponds. White noted that in another part of the island, 'Fernando solaced himself a shoare, with one of the company'. The Portuguese had merely used the ploy of searching for salt to get a day on land! Here we are getting to the bottom of the trouble between the two men. Fernandez was having an affair with one of the women colonists. White is careful not to give any names, but was this why David Glavin was told to go on St John's Island? Was Fernandez amusing himself with Elizabeth Glavin? It would account for Fernandez' truculence, White's silent fury and Glavin's preference of a Spanish prison to being cuckolded daily, and jeered at by the crew. White tells us no more. His spite was only for Fernandez and it was becoming obsessive.

With this interlude on land at an end – an idyll for some – the colonists left the next day resolutely on course for Florida. After nine days' passage they came to what White tells us that Fernandez took to be Croatoan Island. Naturally, since it is White's narrative, it was nothing of the sort. It is doubtful however, if Fernandez was taken in as White suggests. The pilot would have needed to know the latitude to tell him how far south of Roanoke he had made landfall. We have seen the problems of taking such a fix from the moving deck of a ship, but during the time Fernandez was on land, with a clear horizon by careful observation with the cross-staff of the sun it would have been possible to have worked out a reasonably accurate fix. Two shots of the sun at different middays should have been sufficient. With the position known, Fernandez sailed off on a north-easterly course, nearly wrecking the ship on Cape Fear and saved only by Stafford's night watch on the pinnace, 'such was the carelesnes, and ignorance of our Master' – according to White.

At last, on 22 July 1587, and four days after leaving the first landfall, the colonists were off the now familiar Port Ferdinando. Here the *Lion* and the pinnace dropped anchor. For the colonists, who were to make their lives in America, the shoreline with the sloping, sandy beach must have seemed particularly uninteresting. But this was not where they planned to settle; it had been laid down in Ralegh's particular instructions that they should stop at Roanoke to pick up the fifteen caretaker colonists left the year before by Grenville, and then sail round to Chesapeake and make the colony there, leaving the old Roanoke Island settlement abandoned. That, at least, had been agreed and it was an essential part of the plan. Fernandez had other ideas.

White, with forty of the male colonists, transferred to the pinnace, which came alongside the *Lion* to take them to Roanoke Island. No sooner was White aboard the pinnace, than Fernandez called out to the seamen manning the vessel to leave the colonists on Roanoke Island, unless Governor White wished to return, in which case they were to bring him back with no more than two or three of his men. He added that it was too late in the season to sail round to Chesapeake, and all the colonists would have to get ashore here on Roanoke. Though the Portuguese pilot was undoubtedly in charge of seafaring matters, in this instance he was seriously interfering with Ralegh's plan and had usurped White's authority. Fernandez was never sent on another Virginian voyage; he had gone too far, and his action fixed the fate of the colony even before it was ashore. A stronger man than White would have had Fernandez in irons long before and left the navigation to Captain Stafford. White can be blamed for accepting the state of affairs. By now, however, he was as anxious to be rid of the Portuguese as the pilot was to see the last of him. Fernandez' only justification for wishing to be away from Virginia was his desire to catch the *flota* expected in the Azores in August or September, yet he had wasted enough time in the Caribbean. This new turn of events was high-handed and unwarranted on Fernandez' part, and White was foolish to have accepted it; his weakness on this occasion must have undermined further his authority in the colony.

Allowing himself to be ferried over to Roanoke Island with his forty men, White tells us what he found when they landed in the evening light.

. . . at Sunneset, [I] went aland on the island, in the place where our fifteene men were left, but we found none of them, nor any signe, that they had bene there, saving onely we found the bones of one of those fifteene, which the Savages had slaine long before.

With this chilling discovery they settled down uneasily for the night. As they ate their supper, the talk would have been about the fate of the last colonists; Fernandez' insufferable conduct; and the decision to be made about the permanent site of the new colony. First they would have to try to find out what had become of the other fourteen members of the caretaker colony left at Roanoke the previous year. White tells us what followed the next day.

The 23 July, the Governour, with divers of his companie, walked to the North ende of the Island, where Master Ralfe Lane had his forte, with sundry necessarie and decent dwelling houses, made by his men about it the yeare before, where wee hoped to finde some signes, or certaine knowledge of our fifteene men. When we came thither, wee found the forte raised downe, but all the houses standing unhurt, saving the nether roomes of them, and also of the forte, were overgrowen with Melons of divers sortes, and Deere within them feeding on those Mellons: so we returned to our companie, without hope of ever seeing any of the fifteene men living.[3]

There it was. There was nothing to be done so far as any of the missing men were concerned. Sadly, White and his party made their way back to where they had landed the previous night. With Fernandez' refusal to take them to Chesapeake, they would have to make provision for the new settlement, and build cottages so that all the new colonists could be housed at Roanoke Island.

14

'Children Born in Virginia'

Governor White, and those of the Assistants of the governing body of the new colony who were with him that first night on Roanoke Island, accepted the undeniable fact that Fernandez had, with no authority but his own, ordered them to disembark at Roanoke. In accepting this and in deciding to make the old settlement their own they were disregarding Ralegh's instructions. The matter was discussed and decided upon after White's party returned from the old settlement. It was not the sole decision of White himself and clearly he was not alone in disliking and distrusting Fernandez; there was a general disinclination to force Fernandez to carry the colonists round to Chesapeake as he had been engaged to do. It was an important decision because it meant that the colony was failing in one of its principal aims, to provide a safe harbour for privateers. The colonists may have intended to make their way to Chesapeake later, but for the moment White says nothing of that.

Affairs on board the *Lion* had deteriorated so badly as to make it more desirable to stay at Roanoke than face the unpleasantness of forcing Fernandez to carry them to Chesapeake – even though it was only two days' sailing away. Fernandez' reason for not doing so – 'that the Summer was farre spent' – implying that he had not time enough to spare, does not hold water. It was just over a month before the *Lion* sailed, which gave plenty of time to take the colony up to Chesapeake. White, once more, is not telling us enough; in relating little of the circumstances leading up to this momentous decision he may be carefully shielding one or more of his colonists.

White does tell us what happened after they returned from the old settlement: 'The same day order was given, that every man should be imploied for repairing of those houses, which we found standing, and also to make other newe Cottages for such as shoulde neede.'

We are not told when the main party came ashore, but White does tell us that the fly-boat arrived three days after they landed on Roanoke. This is only mentioned because it provoked a sour emotion in Fernandez. He 'grieved greatly at their safe coming: for he purposely left them in the Baye of Portingall, and stole away from them in the night, hoping that the Master thereof, whose name was Edward Spicer, for that he never had beene in Virginia, would hardly finde the place'. Doubtless White was wrong in attributing to Fernandez so diabolical a reason for being grieved, but he was now so biased that the Portuguese could do nothing right. Fernandez always had a very high opinion of his own ability as a navigator and it chagrined him that Spicer, who had never sailed those waters before, should make such a good landfall. Spicer's skill detracted from Fernandez' boastful self-assessment; the latter navigator was displaying professional jealousy. We can take it that the fly-boat was welcomed with joy by the main party, if with ill-humour by Fernandez.

The colonists now numbered 115: seventeen women – two of them pregnant – nine 'Boyes and Children', and the remainder men. The term 'Children' usually indicated those under the age of twelve. From the list of names given by White some deductions can be made. John White brought his own daughter, Elenor Dare, then pregnant, with her husband Ananias, one of the appointed Assistants. If surnames are any clue to relationship then we may include Cuthbert White in the Governor's household, and no doubt servants as well. White and his family would have occupied the largest house, Lane's old dwelling. One can be reasonably certain that Margery Harvie, the other pregnant wife, was married to Dyonis Harvie, another Assistant, and they too would have a substantial dwelling because of his position. Thereafter the only uncertain clues to family groups are surnames. We may deduce that there were two families with children; Arnold and Joyce Archard with a son Thomas; and Ambrose and Elizabeth Viccars with a son named after his father. Of the Assistants, George Howe, John Prat and John Sampson are all associated with children of the same surname – probably sons or younger brothers – and likewise Thomas Ellis, not an Assistant, can be connected with a child Robert Ellis. A final group comprises three men with the same surname, Wyles or Willes. Within the party of thirty-six people were about fourteen family groups. Three names amongst the 'Boyes and Children' – Thomas Humfrey, Tomas Smart and William Wythers – have no name-connection with anyone. Either they were attached as servants to households, were related as step-children to other members of the colony or, least likely, were under the wardship of one of the important male colonists. Six unattached women remain; some may have been servants, or else widows related to others of the men or womenfolk. And finally there is Elizabeth Glane, who may be the deserted wife of David Glavin who left the company so unexpectedly on Puerto Rico. All in all this colony, though only slightly greater in number than the last, required very much more accommodation than the first settlement provided. The joiners and carpenters were kept busy building dwellings and basic furniture with which to equip everyone.

So far the Roanoac Indians had not shown themselves. Weakened by Lane's reprisals after the events of the year before, they had deserted the village on the island and concentrated their remaining numbers on Dasemunkepeuc, the tribal village on the shore of the mainland. The Indians might have suspected that the new colonists would take reprisals for the killing of the caretaker colonist, whose body had been found that first evening, and they kept out of sight until the sixth day of the new colony's existence. It was the end of July and George Howe, one of the Assistants of the governing body, had gone off crabbing by himself, armed with nothing more than a forked stick and, since he was wading in the water, with few clothes on: White says he was 'almost naked'. Howe was so absorbed in his crabbing that he failed to notice a small party of Indians hidden in tall reeds. They were probably hunting deer, wearing deer skins for camouflage – it certainly fooled Howe. He was pierced through by sixteen arrows and, collapsing in the shallow water, had his head beaten in by the Indians' club-swords. The hunting party then made off over the water to the mainland.

White took no immediate retaliatory action, as Lane would have done. This hesitation in taking reprisals may have been in accordance with Manteo's advice: the colonists did not know which tribe was responsible, and to punish the wrong village would only add to their trouble. On 30 July 1587, Edward Stafford and Manteo, with twenty men, took the pinnace down the Sound to Croatoan Island. The Croatoan Indians had always been friendly to the English – they did not have the disadvantage of having to support them, as did the Roanoacs – and they were Manteo's own tribe. The point of the visit was to get news of the vanished fifteen settlers, and to discover who had attacked and killed George Howe. When Stafford landed with his men, the Croatoans, not knowing the purpose of the visit, prepared for an attack. This was a natural reaction in view of their experience. Stafford's reaction was also natural: he ordered his twenty men to load guns and march in formation toward the Indians. The Croatoans behaved as did all Indians when faced with the prospect of firearms: they turned and ran for the cover of the trees. Manteo prevented another disaster by calling out to his tribesmen, who then recognised the landing party as friendly, came out of their forest cover and threw down bows and arrows, some even embracing the colonists. With this moment of tension over, the landing party was carried off to the main village for feasting 'after their manner'.

One of the Croatoans' natural concerns was that they should not become involved in any future skirmishes with the colonists. The previous year, in an event not mentioned by Lane, some of their number had mistakenly been attacked during the skirmish with Pemisapan and one was still badly disabled as a result. To the English, one Indian looked much like another. The Croatoans, for their friendship with the aliens, had suffered much; but notwithstanding the injury Lane had done them, they were forgiving. With an eye to avoiding future errors they discussed with Stafford some means of identifying themselves. On this visit they were told what had become of the fifteen caretaker colonists, which has already been revealed in an earlier chapter. However, 'The next day, we had conference further with them', and the main subject was how to establish friendly relations with the Secotan Indians. It was the Secotan tribe which had been the enemy of Pemisapan four years before; White felt that he could naturally expect them as allies. The Croatoans agreed to pass on word to Secoton, Aquascogoc and Pomeiooc, the villages on the mainland across the Sound, inviting their werowances to visit

White on Roanoke within seven days or to send word of their absence by the Croatoans who likewise would be at Roanoke then. White learnt that it was the Roanoacs who had killed George Howe. The business completed, the Englishmen returned to their base. White tells us that they '. . . came aboord our fleete at Hatoraske'. Hatarask was another name for Port Ferdinando. Just what does White mean? Is he again reporting inexactly? Does he mean, because there were not yet enough houses completed, that some of the colonists returned to the ships and some to the settlement. Or had they all taken to sleeping safely aboard ship after the killing of George Howe? Again, from White's evidence, we cannot tell.

The seven days given to the Secotan villages to send their werowances came and went with no sign of either Secotan or Croatoan Indians. Plainly White had been waiting for these messengers before taking his revenge against the Roanoacs for killing George Howe. At midnight on Monday 8 August 1587 – under a new moon giving little light – White, with Stafford, twenty-three men and Manteo as guide, crossed to the mainland, landing near the Roanoac village of Dasemunkepeuc 'and very secretely conveyed our selves through the woods'. The party went unobserved by the Indians. Concealing themselves in the woods so that the village was between them and the Sound, they watched. They could see a fire burning and around it some Indians sitting, but it was too dark to distinguish if they were in fact Roanoacs. As White relates, 'we presently sette on them: the miserable souls herewith amased, fledd into a place of thicke reedes, growing fast by, where our men perceaving them, shotte one of them through the bodie with a bullet'. But it was another terrible mistake: they had shot one of the wives of a Croatoan werowance! One of the Indians, recognising Stafford, ran calling him by name, and it was realised that these were their friends and allies the Croatoans. Understandably Manteo was distressed, for he had guided the party to attack his own tribe; but he recognised that it was the Croatoans' own fault, even pointing out that, had they come to see White as arranged within the seven days, then the mistake would not have occurred. When all was explained and forgiven it turned out that the Roanoacs, fearing reprisals for the killing of Howe, had deserted their village in a hurry, leaving crops of tobacco, pumpkin, corn and peas. The innocent Croatoans, learning of the abandoned crops had, not so innocently, gone to help themselves without telling White – a stupid and fatal move. Again the long-suffering tribe had paid for their friendship with the colonists by the loss of one of their number.

The following few days were taken up with domestic matters. On the Saturday 'our savage Manteo, by commandement of Sir Walter Ralegh, was christened in Roanoak, and called Lord thereof, and of Dasamongueponke, in reward of his faithfull service'. The Indian had now become a Christian and so would no longer be called a 'savage'. Quite how Manteo took this – or who performed this service – White does not relate. The matter had, in any event, been arranged before the colonists left England and it meant no more than that Manteo became Ralegh's legal feudal sub-tenant of that part of colonial Virginia which belonged to Ralegh by right of discovery. Again, however, White is not telling us what we want to know. The colonists had subscribed on the understanding that they would be allocated 500 acres each in Chesapeake; since they were apparently settling in Roanoke did this mean that they were to be allocated land there instead of at Chesapeake? Apparently not. By the installation of Manteo as lord of Roanoke and Dasemunkepeuc it would seem that the Chesapeake colony was still at the centre of the overall plan. It may have been that a small garrison was to be left in the Roanoke fort when the main settlement was established in Chesapeake.

On 'the 18 [August and a Wednesday] Elenora, daughter to the Governour, and wife to Ananias Dare, one of the Assistants, was delivered of a daughter in Roanoak, and the same was christened there the Sunday following, and because this childe was the first Christian borne in Virginia, she was named Virginia'. Elenor's daughter has earned her place in history as the first English baby to be born in America. Quite rightly Virginia Dare has caught the popular imagination. That Elenor Dare should have boarded the *Lion* when, presumably, she was six months pregnant, to sail across a vast and dangerous ocean to arrive in a completely strange and undeveloped land seems to us quite staggeringly intrepid. It should be remembered, however, that death in childbirth and infant mortality were events of great frequency because of bad hygiene. Whether Elenor Dare had her baby in London or Virginia would have made little difference – she would have expected and received the same very basic treatment in either place – but, since the chance of infection was much greater in London, the likelihood of surviving childbirth was higher in Roanoke. The birth, as White tells us, was followed by a christening on the Sunday in the small chapel on the island. The week after that Margery Harvie had her baby. Unfortunately White told us neither the child's name, nor sex; he simply lists 'Harvye' under 'Children born in Virginia'. The reason for this is that by the time it was christened, on Sunday 28 August, White had left Roanoke.

By now the *Lion* and the fly-boat anchored off shore had been unloaded. A succession of small boats and the pinnace had carried every last box and sack of goods and provisions to land. The ships were careened at Port Ferdinando for breaming and caulking before the Atlantic crossing back to England. There was a slipway at Port Ferdinando, and although its size is not known, it may have been used to haul either or both vessels ashore for the essential breaming. This might account for Fernandez' objection to sailing round to Chesapeake. Once the ships were refloated the small boats began ferrying out fresh water and fuel for the cook-room fires. By 21 August 1587, high water and full moon, the *Lion* and the fly-boat were almost ready to leave. The colonists were writing their last letters home or, as White put it, 'the planters also prepared their letters, and tokens, to send backe to England'. The tokens being mementoes and keepsakes, such as rings or locks of hair, to which the Elizabethans attached a magical significance.

As preparations on land moved smoothly along misfortune struck the *Lion* and the fly-boat at anchor in the seaway. A gale blowing from the north-east subjected the coast to a furious onslaught of gigantic crashing waves and flying spray, pushing the high superstructured ships relentlessly onto the lee-shore. The storm came so suddenly that Fernandez had to cut his cables, and the *Lion* and the fly-boat ran for the open sea, there to beat up and down the coast for six days until the storm had spent its venom. Had Fernandez thought of using this as an excuse to sail for England, he was foiled; in the hurry to make for the safety of the seaway, there had been no time to get all the sailors aboard. With his two ships undermanned, Fernandez had to return to

Roanoke for the men he needed to sail home. We only know from White's account that the *Lion* and the fly-boat were forced to put to sea by the storm. Where was the pinnace? Was she safe in the Sound, careened on the slipway? As with so much of his account White once more lets us down.

With the storm at it height, a controversy had broken out between White and the Assistants. They had decided that two of their number should return to England with Fernandez, but none would volunteer to leave the colony. There was a need for someone in England to organise relief and send them stores that were lacking. Fernandez was, however, an Assistant and he was returning home. Was Fernandez so unreliable? There were three Assistants in England, William Fullwood, James Plat and John Nichols who, once they knew what was needed, would have been perfectly capable of sending it. Finally the whole colony 'came to the Governor, and with one voice requested him to return to England for the better and sooner obtaining of supplies'. John White did not wish to leave the colony because of his daughter and grandchild. Also, being Governor, he felt it was his essential duty to see the colony established. Backwards and forwards went the argument and it reflects badly on White that his colonists were prepared to carry on at a crucial moment of the settlement without their Governor. Outside, the storm lashed and tore at the coast, while inside the atmosphere was just as tense. White was against leaving. In describing these discussions he lets slip another of his ambiguous comments.

[White] alleaged, that seing they intended to remove 50 miles further up into the maine presently, he then being absent, his stuffe and goods, might be both spoiled, and most of it pilfered away in the carriage, so that at his returne, hee should be either forced to provide himselfe of all such things againe, or els at his comming againe to Virginia, finde himselfe utterly unfurnished, whereof already he had found some proofe, beeing but once from them but three daies. Wherefore he concluded, that he would not goe himself.

From White's comment about the party planning to move fifty miles north up the coast it looks as though Roanoke was not planned as the main settlement. To take the distance given as being accurate – which is unwise – this would mean a point on the north shore of the Albemarle Sound. But the statement of distance means nothing and it could be that Chesapeake was intended, some 130 miles north 'into the maine'. The colonists had their boats and could move a distance of 130 miles as easily as fifty. White's evidence, however, remains ambiguous. He fills our minds with useless detail, such as his apprehension about his possessions which had been stolen whilst he was over at Dasemunkepeuc. This does not say much for his daughter's influence, or his authority over the colonists.

This was surely a moment when White should have selected one of the single Assistants and designated his return to England; but no, the argument continued two whole days and nights, and in the end the colonists persuaded the reluctant John White that it would be of more value for him to return home to organise relief than to establish the colony. It also took White two whole pages of his narrative to explain how his better judgement was overcome. A testimonial is included, dated 25 August and subscribed by the colonists, setting out their wish that their Governor should return to England for 'the present and speedie supplie of certaine our knowen, and apparent lackes, and needes most requisite and necessarie for the good and happie planting of us'. By reporting all the detail, White was covering himself against any accusations of deserting the colony.

The matter settled, the colonists swore that they would see to the 'safe preserving of all his goods for him at his return to Virginia'. All White now had to do was wait two more days for the storm to drop. For all White's inexact reporting, we can deduce that the pinnace was also scheduled to return to England. Had it been decided to leave it at Roanoke, White could have returned in it at any time, rather than having to make this urgent and reluctant decision.

On 27 August 1587, Fernandez, who had been riding out the storm, returned from his uncomfortable six days at sea. He gave White half a day to get his baggage aboard the fly-boat, a wise choice of vessel, avoiding the unwelcome company of Fernandez aboard the *Lion*. Typically, White makes no mention of his farewell to the colonists. It was the last time he would see his daughter and his nine-day-old granddaughter, or indeed, any of his colonists. Elizabethans were used to the sharp arrows of misfortune and so the thought that the parting might be permanent would have been in his mind as he said goodbye on the storm-swept beach, littered with the detritus of the recent tempest.

When White went aboard the fly-boat, it had already weighed anchor once and was anchored again further out in the sea-way. Thereafter follows some confusion in White's journal and his dates are not clear. The confusion is the reflection of his having witnessed the most dreaded of sea accidents. The anchor was raised by the capstan on the fo'castle deck, a verticle drum which wound up the cable and was turned by bars pushed round horizontally by the sailors. As the seamen strained round three capstan bars, literally dragging the ship towards the anchor, helped by a small amount of sail for manoeuvrability, one of the bars broke! A capstan running wild in the narrow confines of the fo'castle deck can cut down a crew like a scythe through wet grass, and so it was on the fly-boat. There was a total of only fifteen sailors on board, a small number for a 100 ton vessel: one would have been taking soundings, another at the helm and a third on look-out, leaving twelve to operate the capstan. The accident must have happened at the moment of greatest strain as the anchor was prized from the sea-bed, and the remaining two bars, flying back, must have caught most of the twelve seamen. Unable to jump clear, many of them were injured most severely; White tells us that some never recovered. Those who were able to stand tried to raise the anchor a second time, but were so badly hurt and shaken up that the project was abandoned, the cable cut, and the anchor lost. With over half the small crew out of action, the undermanned fly-boat left the beaches of Virginia. It was poorly equipped to sail the unpredictable Atlantic.

Somehow the fly-boat, limping behind the *Lion*, kept up with Fernandez for three weeks until they reached the Azores, where the Portuguese planned to indulge his passion for privateering. This was completely beyond the capacity of the exhausted crew of the fly-boat, in which only five of the sailors were able to stand up. The letters for home and presumably the tokens were taken aboard the fly-boat from the *Lion* and the former departed from the Azores sustained by loud prayers to God for a safe journey.

The elements were contrary almost from the start. Light winds and calms for twenty days used much of the fly-boat's water supply, which was further depleted by leakages. Then, a fierce north-easterly sprang at the vessel and blew for six days, sending it back over the ground it had made in the previous thirteen days. In a fully-manned vessel a storm is an extremely exhausting experience for all hands, but in the fly-boat with only five active crew the punishment was extreme. Two of the sick died and were buried hurriedly at sea. Most days they could see neither sun, moon nor stars to take a fix with the cross-staff. The lack of drinking water became so acute that 'all the beverage we could make, with stinking water, dregges of beere, and lees of wine which remained, was but 3.gallons, and therefore now we expected nothing but by famyne to perish at sea'. The voyage home to England took on the atmosphere of Coleridge's *The Rime of the Ancient Mariner*:

> With throats unslaked, with black lips baked,
> We could nor laugh nor wail;
> Through utter drought all dumb we stood!
> I bit my arm, I sucked the blood,
> And cried, A sail! A sail!

It was not, however, a sail they found but land, seven weeks and a day after leaving Roanoke. With no means of taking reliable sights, they had no idea what landfall they had made, not that it mattered. It might be France or even Spain – they were at the end of their endurance. It was, in fact, Smerwick in County Kerry, Ireland, on the Dingle Peninsula. They arrived on 16 October 1587. This was the only piece of luck they had on a nightmare voyage, but it came too late for the bo'sun, his mate and the steward, all of whom died aboard the fly-boat within four days of arriving.

Once he had seen that the best had been done for the battered and unfortunate crew of the fly-boat, John White took passage on a boat bound for Southampton. Eight days later he arrived at Hamptone, and there learnt that the *Lion* had preceded him by three weeks at Portsmouth. She had taken no prizes and had arrived in almost as bad a state as his own ship, her crew so weak they had been unable to bring the vessel into harbour. John White, in typical fashion, closed his narrative on 8 November 1587 with a wealth of unnecessary detail, listing the ports he had called at on the way to Southampton, and the names of some, but not all, of those who had died on the *Lion*, leaving us to guess at so many vital matters concerning the colony he had left in Virginia.

15

'Not a Little Distressed'

The complicated plans devised for intensifying the sea war against Spain in the summer of 1587 involved in a small but significant way the Virginian colony. It was to be used as a base by the small flotilla financed by Sir George Carey, the self-appointed 'governor' of the Isle of Wight, whom John White had visited before leaving England. Carey's three privateers, which sailed ahead of White, were the *Commander*, of 300 tons with Captain William Irish; the *Swallow*, a smaller ship of 70 tons; and the *Gabriel*, under half the size of the *Swallow* at only 30 tons. Their mission was to attack and pillage Spanish shipping for their own financial, and England's strategic, gain. They were first reported on 8 June, sailing along the north coast of Puerto Rico. Ten days later, John White had landed at Mosquetal Bay on St John's. With other privateers in the area, the Spanish governor at San Juan, the capital of Puerto Rico, was not having an easy summer. Believing that there was a large English fleet just over the horizon, set on landing and sacking the town, he sent a frantic message for reinforcements, which never came. Captain Irish passed San Juan to wait off Cayo Romano for the Santo Domingo squadron. All he got for his trouble were three frigates of little value. Then off Matanzas harbour, Cuba, he took two more prizes and fourteen prisoners, including a Spanish sailor, Alonzo Ruiz. Though unlucky for Ruiz, this was fortunate for us, because Ruiz tells us something about the rest of the voyage.

Irish, with his flotilla now increased by three prizes, left the Caribbean for the mainland of America making 'their way along the Florida coast until they came to the Bay of Santa Maria in latitude 37°. There they stayed to take in water and found traces of cattle and a stray dark-brown mule.' But what is Ruiz really telling us about the lonely mule and the stray cattle? He made his statement over a year later when he had returned safely home, and his memory might not have been all that good. Certainly 37° is the latitude of Chesapeake, which the Spanish called Santa Maria, but it is very odd that they found livestock there. Perhaps there was a navigational error and Irish was on Hatarask. Ruiz's evidence is uncomfortable: to discover livestock and no colonists is like finding the front door banging uneasily in the wind and the house empty when we had expected to find friends.

Irish would have made for Chesapeake; that is where his instructions would have told him the second colony was to be found. The cattle could not have been taken to Chesapeake by the first colony, since a party only visited Cape Henry on the Chesapeake Bay for a few weeks in the winter of 1585–6 under the 'Colonel of the Chesepians'. The party had gone up the coast in boats which were carried overland for part of the return journey. It is inconceivable that these boats would have been large enough to carry cattle and a mule. The livestock might have been taken there by the second colony, which White had left at Roanoke at the end of August. But we don't know the date of Irish's visit. He was ten days ahead of White at Puerto Rico, then had dallied around Havana taking six prizes and possibly careening his vessels. This means that he would have arrived in Virginia after White, perhaps as late as October. This date allows time for the colonists to transfer their base to Chesapeake. The cattle would have been driven there through forests with no tracks, an impossible undertaking. And why did Irish make no attempt to find the colonists at Chesapeake? Did he not have stores on board for them? All in all Ruiz's account is suspect; it sounds true, yet does not fit what we would expect to find. Plainly, there is something here we have yet to discover.

Irish stayed only three days in Chesapeake, just long enough, as Ruiz tells us, to take in fresh water. From Chesapeake he sailed for England by way of Newfoundland, finally putting into Bristol. Ruiz and his thirteen fellow prisoners were better treated than their English counterparts would have been in Spain. They were put aboard ship for Le Havre to find their own way home, Ruiz eventually arriving in Havana, where he made his report in July 1588. The reservations the Spanish authorities may have had about earlier reports of an English colony in America were swept away by this eye-witness account, which stated, not only that something had been attempted, but its exact location.

By 1587 the Junta de Puerto Rico, a council set up in Puerto Rico to devise Spanish defensive strategy in the Caribbean, had suspected for some time that England had a base in mainland America. The Spanish spy system in England had been seriously inconvenienced when the Spanish ambassador, Bernardino de Mendoza, had been expelled from London in 1584 for meddling in the Queen of Scots problem. For a time, Mendoza's spies had sent reports to him in Paris, where he was based, but, as these reports were gradually picked up by Walsingham's counter-espionage, and false detail transmitted in their place, Mendoza's information became less and less reliable. With the drying up of this useful source, the only other reliable information coming to Spain was from the Caribbean. What the Spanish saw there was alarming. Grenville's fortified camp at Mosquetal Bay, in May 1585, and the information let drop in the subsequent junketings – later confirmed by a prisoner Grenville released in Puerto Rico – had the Junta guessing as to where the settlement was to be placed. The presence in the party of the two Indians, Manteo and Wanchese, led them to believe the mainland north of Florida was the intended location. Menéndez Marqués, with his plans for returning to Spain suspended, had, in December 1585, sent a bark north up the coast to search out the suspected settlement; we know this much from the Frenchman released by Drake at San Agustín. The searching bark did not probe far enough, and turned back 300 miles south of Roanoke. Then came Drake's raid through the West Indies with the puzzling, deliberate taking of the galley-slaves, followed by the sacking of San Agustín before he vanished on a northerly course, as if bound for a base. This brought the first suspicion that Chesapeake might be the site of the English harbour. John White, William Irish, and other privateers passing through the Caribbean in 1587 added to the conviction that somewhere, north of Florida, was a busy English settlement supporting the raids on Spanish property. Until Alonzo Ruiz gave the latitude and the position of what he had seen in Chesapeake, however, Menéndez and the Junta were simply guessing.

November 1587 was the wrong time for John White to have to organise relief ships for his colony. The defence of the country was the principle concern of court and state, and there was little time or resources to spare for the Virginian settlement. It was known that Spain was assembling an Armada to invade England, and in October the Privy Council had ordered a general stay of shipping in English ports to prepare a fleet to fight against the expected attack from the sea. After John White had seen Ralegh on 20 November, however, he tells us that he 'forthwith appointed a pinnasse to be sent thither with all such necessaries as he understood they stood in need of'. The pinnace was due to leave almost immediately and was to be followed, in March 1588, by Sir Richard Grenville with a fleet of seven or eight ships. 'Which Pinnesse [White reports] and fleete were accordingly prepared in the West Countrey at Bidiforde under the chardge of Sir Richard Greenevil.' So far so good; but the pinnace never sailed and nothing more is heard of that part of the relief plan.

The fitting out of the main relief fleet went ahead at Bideford along with all the other preparations to counter the Armada. The Virginian fleet was impressive: the *Galleon Dudley*, 250 tons, to be captained by James Erisey;[1] *The Virgin God Save Her*, the captured prize of 200 tons under Captain John Grenville; the old *Tiger*, now so familiar with the route; and two barks, the *St Leger* and *Golden Hind*, the latter to bring the first news of sighting the Armada. There were also smaller vessels whose names were not given. It is understandable that Grenville should call on his own kin for assistance, Erisey was his cousin, John Grenville his second son, and the *St Leger* was commanded by Grenville's brother-in-law. It is an indication of the importance of the Virginian colony that these needed ships were diverted from the main defensive effort. Before the end of March 1588, Grenville's relief fleet, loaded with stores and probably more colonists, was ready to leave and only waiting a fair wind. All had gone almost too well for White.

But then, on 31 March, the Privy Council realised that valuable ships needed for defence were about to leave, and they sent a hurried order to Grenville that he was not to sail after all. This was confirmed ten days later by more orders of the same intent. The national emergency had taken precedence over the relief of the Virginian colony, and the colonists would have to look after themselves!

Well, not quite yet. John White, whatever his shortcomings as

a leader, was persevering. Grenville's orders were to sail to
Plymouth to join Drake with the ships he needed. The stores for
the colonists were to be taken over to provision the fleet. From
this last minute disaster, White tells us he was able to rescue two
of the smallest ships – the bark *Brave* of 30 tons and the smaller *Roe*
of 25 tons – for the relief of his colonists, although it is more likely
that Ralegh and Grenville were responsible for this move.
Presumably the two ships were too small to be needed by Drake.
The best seamen were involved in the preparation of the fleet,
and the two small vessels appointed to sail to Virginia were
manned by an undisciplined and motley crew.

On 22 April the two barks left Bideford for Virginia: the *Brave*,
captained by Arthur Facy, who had been to Roanoke with the
1586 expedition, and the *Roe* with Pedro Diaz, the unfortunate
Spanish pilot of the *Santa Maria*, captured by Grenville in 1585,
who had very unwillingly been caught up in the Virginia voyages
ever since. After the trouble White had suffered with Fernandez,
it was unthinkable that his services would be needed, and the
tiresome Portuguese pilot was never employed again by Ralegh
even though he was an appointed Assistant. Diaz was a good
enough substitute, though any substitute would have been
difficult for Fernandez to accept. Facy had instructions not to
take the two ships too close to land for fear that Diaz might swim
for shore. In the *Brave* sailed a small party of colonists – seven men
and four women – the women perhaps wives of men already in
Virginia, and the men perhaps with special skills required by the
colony. They were accommodated in temporary cabins on
the upper deck. Below decks were stores for the colony: meal,
biscuits and vegetables – probably vegetable seeds. In the *Roe*
were four more colonists. John White felt vast relief as the *Brave*
cleared the bar at Bideford; he was confident that with God's
good will he would see his family again in July. Typically he
passed over this personal moment with no comment.

By the following day the tone of the venture was set, and it was
not a happy one. Bearing down the coast of Cornwall the two
vessels came upon four ships and, indulging in unwarranted
piracy, chased and boarded them, taking from them only three
men. The next day they behaved no better. They chased and
boarded a Scottish vessel, and another from Brittany, taking from
both 'whatsoever we could find worth taking'. Plainly White had

no control over what Facy got up to on the voyage to Virginia, and seemingly Facy had little control over his own motley crew. Strangely, White, who had been so critical of Fernandez whenever he broke away from the main purpose of the last voyage to go privateering, makes no comment on the worse diversion by Facy. After the two days of pillage and plunder, the 25 April passed without event; but this was made up for later. On 26 April, sighting a sail astern, Facy struck his topsails to lose way, to let the following vessel come up on him. As she drew nearer, he saw she was flying the red cross of St George and so took her to be English. She was nothing of the sort, but was a larger vessel than Facy's and more heavily armed. All hands were called to prepare to fight off the stranger as she made ready to come alongside the *Brave* for boarding. At the last moment the larger ship, a Dutchman bound for the Barbary coast, realised that the *Brave* was English and therefore an ally, and wore off, firing one cannon in salute, to which Facy replied with two cannons. By now it was apparent that Facy would go after any sail that was sighted, regardless of its nationality. Had the Dutchman been less heavily armed and manned Facy would have had her. It was becoming a dangerous voyage for the passengers in the cabins on the upper deck.

On 26 April 1588 heading south in the Bay of Biscay, the *Brave*'s lookout reported a sail to the north-east. It was four o'clock in the afternoon and too late to do much more than shadow the ship through the night. At daylight the victim was sighted, all but hull down on the horizon. The *Brave*, overloaded, was sailing badly and unable to make enough speed to close the gap. It was left to the smaller and faster pinnace the *Roe*, to engage what was now seen to be a hulk of 200 tons bound for Spain. After shots had been exchanged, the *Roe* returned to Facy's ship to take on more men for boarding, in the meantime giving the hulk the opportunity to escape towards the coast of Spain. Another prize had been lost. Trailing out of sight after the hulk, the *Roe* had left the *Brave* at the mercy of any faster-sailing pirate or enemy who might come upon her. If the worst had occurred this would have been rough justice and no help at all to White and his colonists.

Setting course for Madeira in the hope of meeting up with the *Roe*, Facy was overtaken by a well manned and armed man-of-war from La Rochelle. The ships hailed each other in a friendly fashion, before parting with friendly salutes of gunfire. The Frenchman claimed to be bound for Peru. White was suspicious when the stranger fell astern at nightfall; the earlier manoeuvre had obviously been to observe what armament the *Brave* carried. Facy had no alternative but to follow his chosen course as best he could through the night. Next morning, at first light, he saw that the Frenchman had been joined by a tall, heavily armed ship of 100 tons. The latter had taken on reinforcements from the Rocheller during the night and was slowly coming up on the thirty-ton *Brave*, whose fighting crew had been reduced five days earlier by the trans-shipment to the vanished *Roe*. The little *Brave* could do nothing other than sail helplessly on, slowly but surely being overhauled by the raider. With a sinking heart John White watched the Frenchman getting closer and closer. The earlier risks taken in capturing prizes had been bad enough, but here surely was the end of his voyage to Roanoke and reunion with his family.

By two o'clock that afternoon the pursuer was upon its prey. The *Brave* made a tentative but friendly signal which was answered by the wave of a sword. The Frenchman's intent was obvious when she trimmed sail in preparation for coming alongside to board. There was nothing to do but to fight for it. The *Brave* poured the whole of one broadside into the enemy at close range, with some effect: 'with one of our great shot their Master gonners shoolder was stroken away, and our Master gonner with a small bullet was shot into the head. Being by this time grappled and aboord of each other the fight continued without cease one houre and a halfe.'

It was a fearful fight. The French boarding party stormed down over the side, cutting away the anti-boarding nets and carrying all before them as they fought across the soon blood-slippery well of the main deck. Sword, cutlass and pike, pistol and musket clashed above the shouts and curses of the attackers and attacked. From the start the fighting crew of the *Brave* were at a disadvantage in having their decks cluttered by the temporary cabins put up to accommodate the colonists. In addition they were hampered by a number of non-combatants who, preferring to defend themselves in daylight rather than be flushed out from below like hunted rats, came up on deck. There was no clear field of fire or counter-attack area for the defenders, but an hour-and-a-half's hand-to-hand fighting across the decks proves that they did not give in easily. From the first the French knew what they were about and made determined thrusts to capture both poop and fo'castle. With these vantage points gained they turned their pistols and muskets onto the defenders, herded amidships. It was impossible to avoid this murderous fire coming from both sides as the lead balls flew about hitting the unlucky and pitting the wooden decks. As the two vessels ground together in unwelcome embrace, in the Atlantic swell, acts of bravery went unrecorded that summer afternoon. Twenty-three on both sides were killed, and many of the survivors had as many as ten or twelve wounds each. John White was wounded twice in the head, yet again by a pike thrust and finally by a shot through the buttock. Three of his colonists suffered likewise. In the taking of the poop, the master was 'deadly wounded' by a pike jabbed viciously into his face and 'quite through his head'. The mate was in no better shape.

The French, enraged by the loss of so many of their best men, crowded aboard the helpless *Brave*, all set to make a complete massacre of every Englishman they found, until their captain managed to call them off. He did nothing, however, to stop the pillage and ransacking which followed. Everything movable was taken, and White had the agony of seeing his precious stores for the colonists carried up from below and tipped aboard the Frenchman.

With the master and mate so seriously wounded, it seemed essential for the *Brave* to retain the Spanish pilot, Pedro Diaz, to navigate the ship home. Although some of the English made urgent pleas for him to be left, the French were unmoved, and took him away at his own request. But Pedro Diaz did not make a felicitous exchange of jailors. Having promised to land him in the Canaries, the French prevaricated, taking him on to the Cape Verdes. There they threatened to take him with them to the Indies. As they were clearing the Cape Verdes Diaz, by subterfuge, brought the ship close to a small island. Here he jumped overboard and swam for the shore, eventually arriving in Havana; this was three years after his capture by Grenville in 1585.

The *Brave* was left rolling awkwardly in the swell. All she had left was a stock of mouldy ship's biscuits, barely enough for the passage back to England. The English began clearing up the mess of sails, rigging and nets which lay across their decks. White could not help feeling the punishment had been justified by their earlier pirating. Rough justice it was and White, a good Protestant, saw God's work in the day's events. Captain Facy would not have agreed.

That same night the *Brave* set course for England and, left with no guns, cannons or arms to defend herself, crept across the ocean in fear of meeting another enemy. Fifteen days later on 22 May 1588, she arrived in Bideford. White, who tells the story of the voyage, does so without emotion, dwelling on inconsequential details. He concludes: 'Our other pinnesse whose company we had lost before the last cruelle fight, returned home to Cornwall within a few weekes after our arrival, without performing our entended voyage for the reliefe of the planters in Virginia, which thereby were not a little distressed.' Not only were they a little distressed, they were certainly lost.

16

'Anciente Silke'

By the time the despondent John White had returned, it was too late to organise, fit-out and despatch another relief fleet, even had there been no Armada crisis. That same summer of 1588 there were at least two other privateering ventures in the West Indies and the Bay of Mexico, but the ships made no attempt to contact the Roanoke settlement. Since the harbour was intended to be a base for privateers, it is strange that no use was made of it.

Strange, too, that in the whole of 1589 no attempt was made to relieve the settlers. Ralegh and Grenville, the two who could have used their influence to raise some sort of backing, were fully occupied in the excitement of the Armada and its aftermath: Grenville with the impressment of shipping in North Devon and Cornwall, and Ralegh on the high seas in command of three of the Queen's ships, then ferrying troops to Ireland. Once the emergency was over, they both gave their attention to their new estates in Munster, too occupied to think much of the plight of the Roanoke settlers. Perhaps they were content to leave the worrying to John White.

On his return in May 1588, White certainly had a lot to worry about. Concluding that the relief and supply of the 'Cittie of Ralegh' was beyond his energy and the country's means at that moment, he had to use his time, and Ralegh's influence, to find backing for another expedition when the political climate was right. Soon after Ralegh's return from Munster in March 1589 the administrative organisation of the settlement was completely altered by the addition of nineteen London merchants to the Assistants. For the first time the surname of Hakluyt was directly linked with the affairs of the venture. Richard Hakluyt, a cousin of the historian and advisor to the venture since 1584, was among the nineteen new Associates. The three original Assistants based in England were removed, and Simon Fernandez vanished from the account forever. John White and the seven members remaining in Roanoke were retained, and Ralegh, as the main investor, was at the head of the new holding company.

The merchants were headed by the wealthy Customer Smythe, notorious for having made a fortune from buying the right to collect London custom dues. His son, Thomas, would be financially and actively involved in the later Virginian colonies. The merchants were to provide the capital and shipping to send more settlers and supplies vital for the survival of the settlement. In return they were granted rights to trade anywhere within Ralegh's Virginia, free from all taxes for a period of seven years. Ralegh had sold his right to collect dues in return for direct financial support, but the merchants were not philanthropists. Looking back over the sad record of the return on investment since 1584, they may not, for the moment, have felt sufficiently confident to put money behind their signatures, which would explain why nothing was done for the whole of that year. Ralegh's colony was becoming a victim of its own publicity. Early in 1588, as a lure to further investment in the planned 1588 venture, Thomas Hariot had published *A Briefe and True Report* based on his experiences in 1586. He had outlined the advantages of the Virginian colony and revealed none of the disadvantages. This report was republished in 1590, with twenty-eight woodcuts after White's drawings. Hakluyt, the priest and historian, whose enthusiasm and advice had contributed so much to the ventures, published at the end of 1589, his *Principal navigations*, a masterly and inspired collection of English seafaring exploits which included John White's narrative of the 1587 voyage to Roanoke. The public and the new Associates could not claim to be uninformed, but what they read would incline them to believe in a rosy picture of Virginia, a colony where the settlers could well survive on their own. What the new investors failed to realise was that with every day's delay, their investment in the venture was slipping from their fingers.

Although a whole vital year was wasted, the influence and impetus provided by the new Associates showed a dramatic result by January 1590. John Watts, one of the greatest, if not the greatest of the privateer operators of the age, had been engaged to carry new settlers and stores to Roanoke. Three of his vessels were being fitted out in the Thames: the *Hopewell*, of 160 tons, the

Little John, of 120 tons, and a pinnace, *John Evangelist*. This was in essence a privateering expedition with the secondary purpose of calling at Roanoke on the return from the West Indies. At the end of January all three vessels were ready to sail, when an order came from the Privy Council once again staying all shipping. By now Ralegh and John White must have come to expect this regular set-back. The order sent White scurrying to Ralegh asking him to use his influence at court to exempt Watts' three vessels from the general order. The licence was granted by the Queen with the proviso that the settlers and provisions should actually be taken to Roanoke. Watts was bound to this by the sum of £3000: there was to be no repeat of White's last unfortunate experience with Captain Facy. After this interruption the ships were free to sail by the end of February.

But they did not sail at once. There was a brouhaha on the dockside, Watts and his three captains refusing to take White and his settlers with their stores on board the now ready ships. If White is to be believed, this action was in direct disregard of Queen's Orders. It may, however, have been the result of the Governor of Ralegh's inability to assert his authority. With this final drama eventually settled, the vessels at last sailed for Plymouth passing on the way Sir John Carey's lookouts on the Isle of Wight.

Whether or not White paid Carey a visit on this occasion, as he had in 1587, he does not tell us, but someone had been in touch with Sir John. In defiance of the Privy Council order, the *Bark Young* and the *Falcon's Flight,* the former part-owned by Carey, had already sailed on a privateering voyage through the West Indies, intending to call in at Roanoke on their return by the northerly route. The two vessels certainly passed Roanoke, but whether or not they made a stop there is something we are likely never to know.

On 20 March, the *Hopewell* with John White aboard, the *Little John* and *John Evangelist,* sailed out of Plymouth with high hopes of eventually relieving the marooned settlers on Roanoke. John White was looking forward to the joy of seeing his family again.

White once again kept a journal and, although this later narrative is fuller and better than the previous accounts, it is mysteriously lacking in many respects. White begins in his usual bland fashion telling nothing at all of his hopes and fears.

The fift voyage of *Master* John White into the West Indies and parts of America called Virginia, in the yeere 1590.

The 20 of March the three shippes the Hopewell, the John Evangelist, and the Little John, put to sea from Plymmouth with two small Shallops.

The 25 at midnight both our Shallops were sunke being towed at the ships stearnes by the Boatswaines negligence.

On the 30 we saw a head of us that part of the coast of Barbary lying East of Cape Cantyn, and the Bay of Asaphi.

The next day we came to the Ile of Mogador, where rode at our passing by, a Pinnesse of London called the Mooneshine.

The following day they anchored off Santa Cruz. John White has thus carried us uneventfully over 1500 miles, left out important details we should like to have known: what was aboard in the way of supplies, how many new settlers they carried and who these settlers were. He details the inconsequential news of the *Moon-shine* lurking in wait for Spanish prizes, and completely omits to tell us about the *Moonlight,* a ship owned by William Sanderson, one of the wealthy new Associates backing the venture.

The *Moonlight,* of 80 tons, under Captain Edward Spicer, who had been master of the fly-boat on the 1587 voyage, was carrying stores and possibly more settlers. She was also the only ship totally committed to the relief of the settlement. Watts' three vessels, after all, were privateers first and last and theirs was a privateering voyage with the incidental purpose of taking passengers and stores to Roanoke in the *Hopewell.* The *Moonlight* was no privateer, although originally it had been intended that she should join Watts' ships and sail with them from Plymouth. In the event she arrived in Plymouth too late to join the convoy. Rather than risk a lone crossing of the Atlantic, Spicer made an agreement of consortship with the captain of the 30-ton *Conclude.* They would sail together to the West Indies to meet up with John White in the *Hopewell.* Nothing would have been known of this sensible arrangement, or of the *Moonlight*'s part in the plan, if there had not later been a disagreement over the share of prize money, the case being heard in the High Court of Admiralty.

John White's first reference to the *Moonlight* comes suddenly and without mention of the vessel's name. 'The second of July Edward Spicer whom we left in England came to us at Cape Tyburon.'

No explanation is given for this surprise arrival. Had there been another scene at Plymouth? Had Watts' three ships left Plymouth against White's orders to wait for the *Moonlight*? This is likely enough, and to tell the story would have shown John White again unable to assert his authority. His narrative of the voyage is touched with self-pity and the assumption that the crew of the *Hopewell* thought little of him.

The *Moonlight* and its consort the *Conclude* had made a fast crossing of thirty days when, at Cape Tiburon off the western end of Hispaniola, they found three privateers accompanied by three prizes manned by prize crews. According to White there was the usual pillaging and burning through the West Indies, a now familiar spectacle which he and his new settlers endured with patience. It would be another four weeks, however, before they would be on their way to Roanoke, and more patience was going to be needed.

Within hours of the happy rendezvous with the privateers, a Spanish *flota* of fourteen ships was sighted on course for Spain from Santo Domingo. As soon as the Spaniards realised they had an enemy on their trail, the signal was given to scatter and reassemble at Jamaica. The English fleet gave chase, hoping to pick off the slowest ships. The little *Conclude*, being the best and fastest, had left the others behind when by 9 o'clock that evening she sighted a large Spanish ship on a westerly course. The latter immediately altered course to the south-west. The *Conclude* altered course to catch her prey, and at sundown hung a lantern screened to shine aft as a guide to her consorts. Creeping up on the fleeing prize, the *Conclude* sailed through the night with her lookout in the foretop straining his eyes to catch sight of the dim black shape ahead. Finally the ghostly outline of the enemy could be seen from the main deck. The friendly signal on the mainmast was lowered as the *Conclude* crept abeam of the Spaniard. The only sound was that of the sea against the speeding ships. Suddenly the silence was broken by an English voice hailing the other vessel across the gap between them. The answer, when it came, was in Spanish and reassured them that they had their prey right before them. It was the 350-ton *Buen Jesús* under Captain Manuel Fernández Correa, vice-admiral of the *flota* and owner of his own ship. Dropping astern, the *Conclude* hung on to the tail of the Spaniard and, with the aid of the screened lantern, the *Hopewell* and the *Moonlight* were able to find and quietly join their consort. Captain Correa had no sleep that night. The shadows of the three silent vessels coursing in his troubled wake, and the occasional aggressive trumpet calls from the *Hopewell* sounding strangely over the water, left no doubt as to what would follow at daybreak. Against his own nine cannons, the *Hopewell* alone had twenty-two. In the early morning sunlight, the English watched their enemy sailing just ahead of them, her 'Anciente Silke' (or ensign) at the stern, her streamers on the main and foremasts, trailing forward in the morning breeze.

By five o'clock the *Hopewell* had sailed abeam, opening fire on the *Buen Jesús* with muskets – breech-loading swivel guns. The *Conclude*, not wishing to be out of the action, closed the enemy with a shot or two from her falconets. These were only light shots to test the intentions of the enemy, who by then was firing off muskets at anyone to be seen moving on the English ships. The Spaniard's intentions were clear; she was going to fight. The *Conclude* dropped astern, leaving the *Moonlight* and the *Hopewell*, one abeam on the Spaniard's starboard side and the other further aft off the quarter, firing their heavier broadsides into the sides of the high Spaniard to hole the vessel at the waterline. The *Conclude* then came up on the port quarter, firing all her starboard cannon into the Spaniard's side. The three English ships made no attempt to board the enemy, but were content to harass her with their superior broadsides. The sea echoed and re-echoed with the deep explosion of cannon fire and the crack of muskets, while smoke rose from the four grappling vessels and drifted away to the horizon in the south-west. Inevitably, like some large fly trapped by small venomous spiders, the Spaniard had to give in. After more than two hours of hammering, three of the crew of the *Buen Jesús* had been killed and about nine others wounded. She struck sail and surrendered. Immediately the three English vessels sent boarding parties across by boat.

The surrender was taken by Captain Cocke of the *Hopewell*. Then officers and men joined in the general pillage of gold and valuables, while the defeated Spaniards stood helplessly by. The trophies of victory were nicely divided, the 'Anciente Silke' went to the *Hopewell*, the streamer from the mainmast to the *Moonlight* and the forestreamer to the little *Conclude*. But the cargo, when it was eventually brought to London, proved to be one of the most valuable taken for three years: 100 tons of ginger; 6000 hides, (of which about 500 were damaged by seawater in the battle); 200 boxes of sugar; and timber, sugar cane, pepper, cochineal and other spices, finally valued at nearly £6000. For Watts it was a prize worth his captains' while.

After the surrender there was nothing left to do but clear up the debris of battle, bury the dead, put the prize crew aboard and make the *Buen Jesús* seaworthy. No attempt was made to sail after the other members of the *flota;* they had vanished over the horizon in the direction of Jamaica. Only a week later the *Moonlight* and the *Conclude* sighted more *galeones* off the west coast of Cuba, but in waiting for the other members of the small fleet to join them they let these prizes slip away. Then, becalmed, they used the opportunity to land all but nine of the crew and passengers of the *Buen Jesús* on the north coast of Cuba. From these released prisoners and other sources, the Spanish authorities built up a frightening picture of an English presence on their very doorstep. Forty ships had sailed for the Virginian settlement, four of them carrying the women settlers, in one of them the important Governor of the colony. From the Virginian base a fleet of 150 ships was expected to attack the Spanish West Indian bases and *flotas* in 1591. Menéndez Marqués, his chance of a return to Spain now becoming more remote, was a very worried man.

While the *Hopewell* and her two consorts had been engaging the *Buen Jesús,* the *Little John,* the *John Evangelist* and the two small frigates had pursued the *flota.* As the Spanish ships scattered and streamed towards Jamaica, the English vessels were unable to come up with their enemy until just off the island, and by then most of the Spaniards were safe in the harbour of San Juan de la Vega. However, two small frigates, unable to make the entrance to the harbour, ran aground. One the English towed off and secured as a prize. That same evening they picked up three more stragglers. Together the *Little John* and the *John Evangelist* engaged the largest, a *galeon* of 400 tons, and, after broadsides were exchanged, she was boarded. In the violent hand-to-hand fighting across the Spaniard's deck, the captain of the *John Evangelist* lost his right arm and a lieutenant was killed. The English casualties were, in fact, heavy – four men dead and sixteen injured. Even worse, however, the Spaniard, holed beneath the waterline by cannon shot, began to founder and eventually broke up with the total loss of a very valuable cargo. After this severe mauling, the English lost their appetite for further privateering in the Caribbean; they left for the Azores, omitting to keep an agreed rendezvous with the *Hopewell* at Matanzas, off Cuba.

Watts' fleet was by now hopelessly split up. The *Conclude* had become detached from her two companions and, sailing out of the Caribbean, the *Hopewell* and the *Moonlight* with their Spanish prize spent a fruitless few days waiting at Matanzas before the decision was made to head at last for Roanoke. By 31 July 1590, to White's relief, the vessels sailed through the Florida Channel where their prize, the *Buen Jesús,* left them to follow a course for England. With stores and settlers mercifully spared in the dangers of the previous hectic weeks, the English ships were on their way to Virginia and the colonists who had now been abandoned for three long years.

17

'Where our Planters were Left'

The first day of August 1590, found the *Hopewell* and the *Moonlight* battling against the foul weather off the coast of what is now South Carolina. The end of July marks the beginning of the hurricane season, and the thunder, the rain and waterspouts reported by White in his narrative are to be expected, with the revolving storms spinning north up the coast from the Caribbean. For two days the vessels, on a north-easterly course, battled against high winds and seas and, with the current against them, the English must have imagined that the elements were determined to keep them from their goal. By the morning of the third day the centre of the storm had brought calm enough for them to stand into the shore to take a cross-staff shot of the sun as it passed the meridian. The latitude, when they had inaccurately calculated it, was 34 degrees which, if correct, would have put them just south of modern Wilmington. White was getting nearer to his family but was still some 150 miles distant.

By the afternoon the weather had inevitably worsened and it was dangerous to remain close inshore. Putting out to sea, they experienced weather far worse than what had gone before. Hove-to for five days and nights of stinging flying spray and unbearable pitching and tossing, with the decks often nearly vertical, and a darkness of impenetrable rain even at midday, none of them would have been able to sleep. In the crash and roar of the sea, it seemed that their frail vessel would surely turn over and go to the bottom. The daily routine became impossible and yet, to survive, the ship had to be steered and her head kept into the blasting gale. Those at the wheel were lashed to their posts and endured as best they could.

Eventually the winds moved northwards and the calm, when it came, was a heaven-sent respite. The two ships came inshore again to rest, riding high on the heavy ground swell which always

survives a tempest. Red-eyed and weary, the English tumbled
ashore, finding the unmoving ground, the stable horizon and the
quiet strange at first.

For three days they rested, taking on fresh water. Fresh sea fish
was caught in large quantities and brought on board. White
gives their latitude as 35 degrees but he is likely to have been
wrong; they were not that far north and had landed in the area of
the present Cape Lookout on the southernmost of the Outer
Banks. After the merciful interlude of three days' rest, they
weighed anchor and, on the same north-easterly course, sailed
some seventy miles before coming to anchor that night off the
north end of Croatoan Island. The sandy wooded islands were
familiar to White and others on board who had been on earlier
Roanoke ventures. They were getting very near indeed to the
colony, only fifty miles away.

The next morning soundings were taken from the ships' boats.
This was a necessary precaution; White would have remembered
the *Tiger* being all but lost off Wococon in 1585. During the
following days the English made painfully slow headway. By 15
August they were off the southern end of modern Bodie Island,
and Roanoke was but fifteen miles distant. At least by their slow
progress they were advertising their presence to anyone ashore. It
was the evening of 15 August when they came to anchor. Over
the trees of Bodie Island, which they called by the Indian name
Hatarask, they saw to the north-west, over Roanoke, a great pall
of smoke hanging motionless. That night John White went to
sleep contented, for he believed the smoke to be a signal from
colonists who 'were there expecting my return out of England'.

White was possibly not the only one who slept contented; there
were others who had reason to. John Spicer, who had been with
the 1587 expedition, had with him in the *Moonlight* John Taylor
and Edward Kelly who had been to Roanoke in 1585-6. Also in
the *Moonlight* were Robert Colman and Henry Millett who with
John Taylor all had the same surnames as certain members of the
1587 colony. It is stretching fact too far to say that these men were
relatives of the 1587 colonists, but they could have been, and
therefore might have been as keen as John White to see the
colonists of 1587 again.

The next morning, with full expectation of meeting up with
the marooned colonists, two boats were got ready to take ashore

John White, Edward Spicer and Abraham Cocke, the captain of
the *Hopewell*. Before the party left, the master gunner of the
Hopewell was ordered to arrange for special signal guns to be fired
off throughout the day to attract the attention of anyone within
earshot. The two ships were anchored some nine miles off shore
and the two boats were only about halfway over when 'we saw
another great smoke to the Southwest of Kindrikers mountes'.
Believing this to be another signal from the colonists, White
decided to land on the Outer Banks and walk down the island to
contact whoever was making the smoke. Today it is impossible to
follow the same path taken by White and his party; the banks
have shifted and have been breached by the sea so that what was
once a continuous stretch of wide, tree-covered land is now a
narrow succession of broken islands or sand hills running south
from Port Ferdinando – where White landed – to the then Cape
Kenrick, with Kenricks Mounts close by. Cape Kenrick was
abeam of the modern town of Salvo, and in a position now
fathoms deep beneath the sea some four miles due east.

It is very difficult to judge the distance of smoke on the horizon,
and the smoke White, Spicer and Cocke sought proved farther off
than expected. As they walked along the sand at the edge of the
beach, they seemed to be getting no closer. They half expected to
see one or some of the colonists coming along the beach to meet
them, but their hopes declined as the distant thud of the signal
guns became fainter and fainter. At last the trio reached the
source of the smoke. Before them was nothing but a blaze started
by the sun in the tinder-dry grasses. There was no sign of human
habitation. Their disappointment was aggravated by their
fatigue from having walked so far along the shifting sand.
Moreover, there was no drinking water to be found here or at any
place along the return journey. Tired and aggrieved they arrived
back at the boats they had left earlier that morning. The sailors
who rowed them ashore had not, meanwhile, wasted their day.
They had returned to the ships for empty water casks and, after
digging around in one of the dunes, had found a handy supply of
drinking water to fill the casks. It was now too late to think of
going on to Roanoke Island. Exhausted, the boat party returned
to the ships.

Early next morning, 17 August 1590, John White was up and
ready to be off again. In the *Moonlight*, however, Edward

Spicer had risen earlier to send one of the boats ashore for more drinking water, and it was ten o'clock before White and his landing party were ready to leave. In giving us this detail White is being careful to absolve himself from any blame for what followed – the delay was not of his making. By now the two ships had moved closer inshore and were lying only two miles from the line of heavy surf beating ceaselessly on the beach. This was an anchorage that needed careful watchkeeping, for to be caught so close to a lee shore would be dangerous when it really came on to blow. White was halfway across before Spicer got his boat away, and it was White's boat which discovered first the danger of the passage between the islands into the Sound beyond. The wind was freshening from the north-east and the tide was now running out very strongly over the sand bar; an earlier landing would have avoided the racing currents of brownish water flecked with sinister, cinnamon-coloured foam, now pouring out of the Sound into the sea. The north-east wind blowing strongly from seaward was forcing the waves back on themselves, resulting in a very troubled sea, with waves suddenly building up and coming from every direction. White's boat had all but passed through the breaking water and was having an uncomfortable time, when one wave, bigger than the rest, broke over the boat, half filling it with water, spoiling arms, powder and the day's victuals. It was only by careful steering, furious bailing and the sailors' strength in rowing the now desperately heavy, water-logged boat that no lives were lost. With their boat pulled up onto the beach within the Sound, White's party watched with apprehension as Edward Spicer brought his boat through the same hazardous water.

Edward Spicer unwisely came into the racing tide with his mast stepped, which tended to make the boat top-heavy. Unwiser still, the helmsman was unskilled in managing a boat in shallow water. They were doing well however, until halfway across a heavy, dangerous wave broke over them and the boat overturned, throwing all out into the sea. Like so many sailors, most of Spicer's men were unable to swim. Those who clung to the upturned boat as it was swept seawards were lucky until, passing over the bar, the boat was beaten down into the sand. Shaken loose from their fragile hand-hold, the sailors fell back into the seething foam. Others, attempting to wade ashore, were swept off their feet and away out into the open sea. Two or three times more the boat was turned over as it was tossed about like a stick. Edward Spicer and his helmsman were washed out into the Atlantic with five of their shipmates and were seen no more. Four who could swim kept themselves afloat until, in shallower water, they were rescued by four of those from the beach. Amongst those drowned were Edward Kelley, who had been with the 1585 colony, and Hans the surgeon, who may have been Hans Walters of 1585.

The upturned boat was salvaged by the shore party, who launched their own craft in a vain attempt to help their drowning companions. There was no great desire on the part of the rescued or rescuers to continue across the Sound to Roanoke. It was only by the urgent persuasion of John White and Abraham Cocke that the sailors were prevailed on to row further. White reports: 'Seeing the Captaine and me so resolute, they seemed much more willing.' So the two boats were got ready and the party, now numbering nineteen, rowed over the Sound to Roanoke in the failing evening light. They were making for Shallowbag Bay 'but before we could get to the place, where our planters were left, it was so exceeding darke, that we overshot the place a quarter of a mile'. As they realised their mistake they 'espied towards the North end of the Iland ye light of a great fire thorow the woods'. How White's hopes must have risen at the sight of the distant fire glowing through the trees! Rowing hard towards the light, they arrived off the site of the fire and dropped a grapnel to hold the boat off the shore as they debated the safety of venturing on the land. These might be unfriendly Indians. Caution won, and for some time, with the light of the fire reflecting red on the surface of the water, they played trumpet calls and English tunes familiar to the colonists. There was no answer from the woods save the empty echo of the trumpet from the flickering shadows of the trees silhouetted against the firelight.

At daybreak they landed. As John White strode across the sand of Roanoke that he had left three years before, did he already realise that this was not where he would again meet his family? Possibly he did; the omens had not, so far, been good. Coming to the fire he and his party had watched through the night he found 'the grasse & sundry rotten trees burning about the place'. There was no camp fire, no colonists, not even an Indian camp. This was another hollow joke played by nature – a fire started by natural causes.

Still affected by the disaster of the day before, their hopes dashed by the empty fires, White, with Abraham Cocke and a few others, walked dejectedly two miles across the width of the island. No doubt they discussed the lack of response by the colonists to their arrival. If the colonists were still on the island, they could not have failed to notice the two vessels at anchor beyond the bar, or to have heard the signal guns. By now it was perfectly clear to White that his colonists were no longer on Roanoke and his purpose in walking across the island was to make contact with the local Roanoac Indians. He and his men came out of the woods on the west side of the island at a point directly opposite the mainland village of Dasemunkepeuc. They neither saw nor met any Indians and, at the water's edge, turned north-west to take the way back along the beach round the north end of the island. At one point they saw footprints in the sand which had been made the night before by Indians – Indians who had learnt the bitter lesson of the superior power of the English, and who had wisely either left the island or were watching from the safety of the woods.

White and his party followed the shoreline right round the top of Roanoke, past the deserted outpost now called Fort Raleigh, which White does not mention, down the island past the place where they had landed that morning and on to where John White knew the old site of the colony to be. Nearing the spot, they saw on a tree growing conspicuously on top of a dune 'curiously carved these faire Roman letters C.R.O.'. White now explains that, before he left the colonists in 1587, it had been arranged that when they moved from the old settlement to a new site they would indicate where they had gone by carving the name of the place on trees, posts or doors; if in some danger they would carve a Maltese cross over the name.

Here, for the first time, White had evidence of his colonists. There was no Maltese cross indicating any danger, but the three letters were not a word. Whoever had begun cutting the name had never finished! This, at least, was something to give hope and what followed is best told in White's own unemotional words:

We passed toward the place where they were left in sundry houses, but we found the houses taken downe, and the place very strongly enclosed with a high palisado of great trees, with cortynes and flankers very Fort-like, and one of the chiefe trees or posts at the right side of the

entrance had the barke taken off, and 5. foote from the ground in fayre
Capitall letters was graven CROATOAN without any crosse or signe of
distresse; this done, we entered into the palisado, where we found many
barres of Iron, two pigges of Lead, four yron fowlers, Iron sacket-shotte,
and such like heavie things, throwen here and there, almost overgrowen
with grasse and weeds.

John White stood in the compound of the forlorn and deserted
settlement. Around him was the palisade which he had been
surprised to find. Before him lay evidence of the dismantled
houses, overgrown with weeds. It was obvious to him that the
colonists had left over a year ago, perhaps in a hurry. He heard
the soughing of the wind in the trees beyond the enclosure, the
nervous rustle of squirrels in the leaves of the woods which are
never still, the distant cry of a jay. Here White's little grandchild,
Virginia Dare, had lived for a short time; here, Elenor, his own
daughter had lived too. The area around him had once heard the
sound of English voices discussing, arguing where the colony
should go. But the upright timbers of the palisade were mute and
told White nothing more than 'CROATOAN'.

Walking puzzled and disconsolate from the deserted
compound, White and Cocke went 'by the waterside, towards
the point of the Creeke to see if we could find any of their botes or
pinnisse, but we could perceive no signe of them, nor any of the
last Falkons and small Ordinance which were left with them at
my departure from them'. They were walking along the beach of
Shallowbag Bay from the direction of Baum Point towards
Dough's Creek – 'the poynt of the Creeke'. The path they
followed is now beneath the marshy area at the north end of the
bay.

As they turned back from Dough's Creek, they were met by a
party of excited sailors coming to find them. The seamen, with
nothing much to do, had occupied their time looking around for
evidence of the colonists and had found some chests broken open
with the contents scattered around. They led White and Cocke to

the place, which was in the ende of an olde trench, made two yeeres past
by Captain Amadas: wheere wee found five Chests, that had been
carefully hidden of the Planters, and of the same chests three were my
owne, and about the place many of my things spoyled and broken, and
my bookes torne from the covers, the frames of some of my pictures and
Mappes rotten and spoyled with rayne, and my armour almost eaten

through with rust; this could be no other but the deede of the Savages our enemies.

In his account John White is telling us of what surprised him: the high palisade around the site; the dismantled houses; the paraphernalia left on the ground, too heavy to transport, though some of the falcons and small guns had obviously been moved away; his chests, which the colonists had promised to keep safe; above all the indication that the colonists had left for Croatoan. But White, although clear enough about the destination of Croatoan, is confusing his other facts. In referring to the old trench 'made two yeeres past by Captain Amadas', he has forgotten that Amadas was last at Roanoke Island in 1586! And in another part of this same narrative he reverts to his previous comment that the colonists were planning to move fifty miles after he left so unwillingly in 1587, whereas Chesapeake is 130 miles distant from Roanoke Island (unless he was hazy about the distance of a place he had never visited). Nevertheless, Croatoan Island had never been considered a suitable site for the colony.

Far from being discouraged by what he found, White was 'greatly joyed that I had safely found a certaine token of their safe being at Croatoan, which is the place where Manteo was borne, and the Savages of the Island our friends'. It only remained for John White to go to Croatoan.

White and his party did nothing more on Roanoke Island. By the time they had finished searching through the debris of the broken chests and sifting through the sand in the hope of finding something, it was evening and the sky was becoming overcast – a well-known sign of bad weather to come. Taking a last look at the old settlement, they left and got themselves back on board with difficulty, for the wind had risen and with it the sea. It was another uncomfortable night aboard the two vessels, added to which it was feared that the force of the wind and sea would cause the anchors to drag or the cables to part. They lasted out until daybreak, however, when captain Cocke of the *Hopewell* sent a boat ashore, manned by five sailors who could swim, to pick up six seamen marooned overnight after having been left to fill water casks. The sea was now so rough that it was not possible to bring back the filled casks. Yet another night, which White classified as very stormy and foul, was passed off shore. The wind, luckily, was not yet blowing from seaward and there was no danger of being driven on to a lee shore.

In the grey, early light of the second stormbound morning White persuaded Cocke to sail for Croatoan, where it was supposed that they might find the lost colonists. Cocke had been holding on in the hope of the weather letting up enough to allow the water casks to be retrieved. The wind was with them for a southerly course and there was little point in remaining anchored off Roanoke. However, in weighing anchor, the cable parted and the *Hopewell* was driven towards Cape Kenrick. They let go a second anchor which like the first was immediately lost. Had they not had the good fortune to find themselves in a deep channel of water running close to the Cape, they would certainly have been driven on to the shore and wrecked. By good seamanship and a certain amount of luck, Cocke got his ship clear of danger and into safer, deeper water further out to seaward, but it had been a close thing and they now only had one anchor left. Moreover, the weather was worsening and clearly it was not possible to make Croatoan.

Food on board was running low after five months at sea and with some of their water casks left ashore they were not well victualled. A hurried conference between White and Cocke brought the proposal that they should head south with the wind to the West Indies for provisions, winter there and return to Croatoan in the spring. The plan was unusual but its attraction was the possibility of taking more prizes. Democratically, the members of the crew were consulted and, with the prospect of more prizes in view, they unanimously agreed. It only remained to consult John Bedford, who had succeeded Spicer in the *Moonlight* after his drowning. His ship, he claimed, was not sound enough to continue for so long a voyage. This was not altogether true, but Bedford and his crew may have been anxious to assert their claim in England for prize money at the earliest opportunity. That night the two ships parted company, the *Moonlight* sailing for England and the *Hopewell* on course for Trinidad.

John White is the only source for the continued voyage of the *Hopewell*. It may well have been that Cocke intended to return to Croatoan in the spring, although White tended to show himself as having made that decision and influenced Cocke to agree to it. The fact is that the *Hopewell* did nothing of the sort.

The weather which had conspired against White since his arrival off Florida now blew the *Hopewell* off course, and with the wind veering round to the west, the ship was forced to run before the seasonal gales with only the fore-course set. This effectively closed the option to make Trinidad and, according to the demon of the tempest, White decided to set course for the Azores and thence for England. The demon, however, had not yet finished its work. From the dangerous blasts of gales the *Hopewell* was now delivered into flat calms and light winds, which were perversely followed by more gales. There was seemingly no meteorological middle course. At last, on 17 September 1590, sighting Corvo and Flores, the two western islands of the Azores, White and his crew attempted to make harbour at either one or the other of them. Due to light contrary winds it took two whole days to reach an anchorage on the north side of Flores. They narrowly missed the *Moonlight* which slipped away for England as soon as the *Hopewell* was sighted. Here they met up with Sir John Hawkins and Sir Martin Frobisher, who shared the conviction that Spain could be beaten by blockading the treasure fleets coming to Spain from the Indies. The Queen had sent both adventurers into the Atlantic with a fleet to prove their point. Even as the *Hopewell* was making for Flores, Menéndez Marqués, so long detained in Florida, was at last landing in his own country with a treasure fleet, after running through Hawkins' blockade.

On 1 October 1590, the *Hopewell* found a fair wind to take her to England and made Plymouth by 24 October, not many days behind the *Moonlight*. Yet again White had returned from a fruitless voyage in search of his family, and the lost colony.

Another man would have been more successful in his mission than White.. It is his tragedy, and that of the lost colonists, that he should have failed where a stronger character might have succeeded. Finding himself in a difficult and uncongenial position, he always endeavoured to do his best – he was honest and he cared – but he was an artist who should have been left to his easel. We last hear of him in Newtown, County Cork, in Ireland, writing to Richard Hakluyt on 4 February 1593 (Hakluyt published the letter in the 1600 edition of *Principal navigations*): 'I take my leave from my house in Newtowne.' We may imagine John White still mourning his vanished daughter and grandchild, back at work with his brushes.

White may have made a final attempt to reach his family in 1602. For with Martin Pring a John White, on board a privateer the *Susan Parnell*, was transferred off Cuba to the *Archangell*, captained by Michael Geare. Geare was one of John Watts' men who had captained the *Little John* in 1590 in White's earlier attempt to rescue his colony. Geare put Pring and White in charge of a Spanish prize to be sailed home to England. The ship was under-victualled and leaking badly. Apart from calling at Campeche Bay in Yucatán, there is no record of other ports of call until she barely made Morocco.[1] But was this our John White and did he call at Roanoke Island? We simply don't know. But even in 1602, the colony still lived on.

18

'A Whole Country of English'

From John White's account of what he found at the old Roanoke settlement in 1590, it is possible to make some sort of reconstruction of the events following his departure in 1587.

Within a short time of John White's departure, the colonists would have made their decision on the permanent site of the colony, and the move would have taken place that autumn. White, it will be remembered, mentioned two alternative sites. The more sensible one was that recommended by Hakluyt and Lane, on the southern shores of Chesapeake Bay – a site specified by Ralegh in the instructions for the founding of the 'Cittie of Ralegh'. The other was given in White's odd throw-away comment, '50 miles into the maine', which would have been the area up the Albemarle River, explored by Lane in 1585. The Albemarle, however, would not have provided the urgently needed base for shipping, and one would be tempted to dismiss this as a possible site were it not for the strange fact that, much later, small groups of colonists were reported as being in both areas.

Expecting White to return to Roanoke in the summer of 1588 with the much needed supplies and more colonists, the settlers would have left a holding party of perhaps no more than a dozen men behind the heavily fortified palisade at Roanoke, to guard the heavier equipment, and to keep White's chest safe against his or the main party's return. They would have been there to welcome White, and to guide him to the new settlement. Most of the colonists would have departed from Roanoke in the pinnace and all but one of the smaller boats, taking with them the dismantled houses, the falcons and smaller guns – all of which White noted as having gone. Although they would have needed to make more than one journey to accomplish the transfer, they nevertheless left behind the heavier equipment which White noticed lying about inside the compound.

Behind their stockade, the holding party waited in vain for White's return in the summer of 1588. For some reason the main party did not send down for the heavier equipment: perhaps their pinnace was wrecked, although they could have built another. Finally, despairing of White's return, the old site was abandoned in favour of the friendly Indian village at the south end of Croatoan Island. Other reasons – lack of food perhaps or hostile Indians – could, however, have compelled the departure of the holding party; the unfinished word CRO suggests a hurried evacuation. Taking the small boat left to them, the few settlers would have been unable to carry with them the heavy chests, iron bars, lead pigs or the remaining falcons, but they did leave their destination carved on the gate post of the palisade to guide John White or any returning party.

The new base on Croatoan was about twenty-five miles south of Roanoke and south-west of the modern town of Buxton. From there it would have been simple to post lookouts on the seaward side of the island to watch for English ships and for White's arrival. Here the holding party settled down amongst their Indian friends to wait. White, however, did not return until 1590, and by then the holding party had gone. Unfortunately no one ever returned to Croatoan to search for the settlers, and where they went remains an unanswered question. Their likely goal was to reach the main party of colonists.

Since White and his party were in the area of Roanoke for a total of three weeks – ample time for friendly Indians in Croatoan to send word of two ships to the main colony, and for a party of colonists to return – why then did nobody come to White on Roanoke? Manteo and his tribe may perhaps have moved away from Croatoan, and if hostile Indians were there they would have done nothing but wait for White and his party to leave. The movements of the Indian tribes at this time are unknown. During the year that Lane passed in the area there were upheavals enough. Who can say what had passed since White last saw his colonists three years ealier? Manteo and his tribe could have been wiped out along with the holding party, or they could have joined the main colony. But this is only speculation, although we can be certain – as will be shown – that the main colony was still in Virginia when White was on Roanoke in 1590.

The Spaniards must have the final word on this subject.[1] The
Duke of Medina Sidonia, ordering the organisation of the
Armada, was not too busy to ponder on the threat of an English
base in Virginia. In March 1588 he sent orders to Menéndez
Marqués, the energetic Governor of Florida, that Marqués
himself must go to look for and eliminate the Virginia colony.
The Duke was either too short of shipping or else chose to
overlook the point, but he failed to send to Menéndez Marqués
ships or soldiers to execute the command. Dutifully, Marqués
waited for reinforcements or even instructions on how the
expedition was to be achieved, but no word came. At last he sent,
on his own initiative, a small vessel north from Florida with a
pilot who knew the coast.

On 28 May 1588, a *barca luenga*, a small ship which could be
sailed or rowed, left San Agustín with a pilot and twenty-eight
men under the command of the governor's nephew. North they
went, without looking into the inlets of the Outer Banks, to
explore the shores of the southern Chesapeake. That they found
nothing does not indicate that the main English colony was not at
Chesapeake but that the settlement was not close to the shore –
possibly it was inland up a long creek. The Spanish made an
astoundingly quick exploration of the area, mistakenly looking
for a large and flourishing colony. Chesapeake was the farthest
they penetrated and, having satisfied themselves that there was
nothing to be seen on its shores, they started back, running down
the coast before a freshening northerly wind. The breeze blew up
into a storm, however, causing them to shelter in Pamlico Sound
behind the Outer Banks. Here they found 'a slipway for small
vessels', and on land a number of wells made with English casks,
and other debris indicating that a considerable number of people
had been there. The Spaniards had blundered on one of the
points on the Banks at Port Ferdinando which the colonists had
used as an intermediate station between Roanoke and ships
anchored off shore. The slipway was useful for the repair of boats
and the pinnace. They looked no farther, for they had found
what they thought was the evidence they had been sent for, and
returned to San Agustín. No doubt they had been watched from
a distance by the holding party of colonists. Their discovery tells
nothing about the position of the colony in early July 1588.

After White's abortive voyage of 1590, further attempts were

made to contact the lost colony, but our knowledge of them is
sketchy. Unfortunately they were not included in the last edition
of Hakluyt's *Principal navigations*, published in 1600, and Hakluyt
is our only source of certain information up to 1590. In 1595
Ralegh planned to return to England from Guiana by way of
Virginia, but failed to do so – indeed his efforts to relieve the
colony appear half-hearted. In 1602, however, he despatched
Samuel Mace to Virginia. Mace was said to have been 'at
Virginia twice before; and was employed by Sir Walter Ralegh to
find those people which were left there in the yeere 1587'.[2]
Samuel Mace may have found the colony on one of his earlier
voyages, but they are unrecorded. On this voyage he made no
attempt to go near Roanoke or Chesapeake. Landing somewhere
between Cape Fear and Cape Lookout, he and his party spent a
month collecting plants before returning home. If Mace had
already found the colony on one of his earlier voyages, and had
seen that the colonists were self-sufficient and unwilling to return
to England, he probably would not have felt the need to visit
them frequently.

On 5 September 1603, the year of James's accession to the
throne of England and of serious plague in London, three
'Virginians' were seen propelling themselves in a canoe on the
Thames before Cecil's great house overlooking the river and
fronting on the Strand.[3] How these Indians arrived in England
has never been properly explained. Samuel Mace was, perhaps,
responsible, for early in 1603 he was again sent to Virginia by
Ralegh to reconnoitre Chesapeake in preparation for the
Jamestown settlement. By the time Mace returned, Ralegh was
in the Tower, trapped by Cecil's cunning. With other more
pressing concerns on his mind, Ralegh's interest in his Virginian
lost colony ceased.

Bartholomew Gilbert who sailed in Ralegh's service early in
1603, covered the American coast from Cape Fear to New Jersey.
He even passed the entrance to Chesapeake Bay. Chancing to be
ashore on Delaware Bay he had the bad luck to be attacked and
killed by Indians. His ship returned too late in 1603 to have
transported the three 'Virginians'.

Even these sketchy details are enough to show that there
probably was contact with the lost colony after 1588, most likely
through Samuel Mace. Certainly King James and his privy

council believed the colony to exist. The year 1604 was celebrated for the end of the long and unnecessary war with Spain. By the time the terms of the treaty were drawn up and agreed in London, both the Spanish and the English appear to have been in possession of information – which has since been lost – regarding the continued existence of the colony. It was common knowledge in London too. In September 1605 the Children of the Queen's Revels at Blackfriars, performed a play called *Eastward Ho* by Ben Jonson and two fellow playwrights. It was a witty and amusing piece. Captain Seagull, passing his time ashore in a riverside inn, tells of the wonders of Virginia: 'A Whole Country of English is there man, bred of those that were left there in '70 [sic]; they have married with the Indians and make them bring forth as beautiful faces as any we have in England.' Even the chamber-pots, he claimed, 'were of gold'. The survival of the lost colony was obviously well known to Jonson, and it had become tavern talk.

So the colony lived on, most likely on the southern shore of Chesapeake Bay, in the territory of the Chesepian tribe. To have achieved peaceful co-existence with the Indians, the colonists must have been self-sufficient in food – a lesson learned at Roanoke. Their particular skills in working metals would have been of enormous advantage to their Indian friends, who would have benefited, too, from the technology of the wheel and the skill of throwing pots.

By now a new generation of colonists would have grown up, the Harvie child and Virginia Dare having reached the age of twenty. In twenty years a great deal could have been achieved under an energetic leader: ships could have been built to export surplus agricultural products such as corn, tobacco and wine; minerals could have been mined and timber exported. Since none of this happened we can infer that Indian wars and disease had kept down the numbers of the colony, and those who intermarried with the Indians had adsorbed too many of the Indian customs to allow the colony to progress dynamically. We can dismiss any idea of a bustling English settlement as pictured in Captain Seagull's imagination. We must look, instead, for the usual Indian community, but one with houses of better construction, built of timber felled in the woods by axes and shaped by saws. They would have had a forge turning out ploughshares, axes, knives and swords for their own use and for trading with neighbouring tribes. The fields surrounding the village would have been ploughed by horses or oxen, producing little more than was adequate for the colonists. Cattle may have grazed in enclosures and, within the village, pigs and poultry, including turkeys, scratched around in the dust for scraps. The Christian beliefs of the colonists would have survived; but the ceremony enacted in the village chapel would have been influenced by some of the Indians' ways.

To the west of Chesapeake the neighbouring tribes had fallen into the power of a ruthless and despotic chief, Powhatan, of whom the Chesepians remained independent. In 1604 or 1605 an English ship had sailed into the bay and kidnapped several Indians from one of Powhatan's subject tribes.[4] This is likely to have been the last time that an English ship visited Chesapeake before the Jamestown settlers arrived. The kidnapping was not forgotten by Powhatan. Did the colonists suspect that they could be the objects of Powhatan's revenge and that they were only living on by the goodwill of the powerful chief?

On 26 April 1607, Captain Christopher Newport reached Cape Henry at the entrance to Chesapeake Bay. Out at sea a storm was brewing; ashore in the colony, although early, the day's work would have already begun. The women would have been seeing to the poultry and to the milking of the cows, whilst the menfolk went hunting or fishing. Golden–brown children perhaps played in the dust of the village. Christopher Newport in the *Susan Constant*, accompanied by the *God Speed* and the *Discovery*, had arrived in Chesapeake after a troublesome voyage from England lasting four months. His arrival at that moment was something of an accident. With 144 settlers aboard, his fleet was bound for colonial Virginia to found a new colony at Jamestown on the James River which ran into Chesapeake Bay. Had it not been for the storm blowing up in the Atlantic they would have sailed past the entrance to Chesapeake in complete ignorance of their true position. Running into the bay for shelter against the storm, they stumbled on their destination.

The three vessels came to anchor off Lynnhaven Bay on the southern shore of Chesapeake and almost immediately Captain Newport, four other gentlemen and a party of about thirty sailors set off for the shore to get their first taste of a world which was to be their future home. Disappointingly they found 'nothing worthy of speaking of' but, after so long at sea, the green of the countryside, the low hills and wooded slopes were seductive, and they tarried ashore until darkness began to creep upon them. They saw no living soul. No lost colonists came running to them, and no Indians either, until they turned to go back to the boats on the beach. As they sauntered back in groups toward the shore, five Indians burst from the cover of the ever-rustling woods carrying bows between their teeth. Racing across the open ground towards the astonished Englishmen, stopping only to let off arrows, they finally 'charged us very desperately in our faces'.[5] One of the sea captains was wounded in both hands and a sailor seriously injured. It was only when the attackers had exhausted the arrows and the attacked had managed to let off their firearms that the Indians returned to the woods making belligerent cries. These were Powhatan's men on the war path. To have attacked such a large party known to be armed with guns showed a great deal of courage. The English returned to their ships in some excitement, well aware by now that their visit was unwelcome.

Unwelcome they were indeed. Their arrival either provoked or coincided with Powhatan's decision to exterminate his neighbours the Chesepians, and the lost colony with them. Powhatan had taken seriously prophecies from his priests that 'from the Chesapeack Bay, a Nation should arise, which would desolve and give end to his Empire'.[6] This was not the first time that the despotic Powhatan had acted on such a prophecy. The Indian chief and his allies attacked the Chesepian Indians, easily outnumbering them and overrunning their villages. The entire Chesepian tribe was wiped out, together with the colonists. Powhatan's men slaughtered all the colonists they could find, sparing none. Those who tried to escape were chased into the woods and killed there. The villages were set on fire and the crops burnt: the busy communities of the morning had ceased to exist by that evening. Powhatan was eliminating one enemy in the face of another 'from the Chesapeack Bay'.[7]

On the days immediately following their arrival in Chesapeake, the English made more explorations, never meeting with anyone, but occasionally finding deserted cooking fires. In the distance they saw 'great smoakes of fire'. It was smoke from the burning villages and crops of the Chesepian Indians. The

English seemed to be aware of something going on around them, some unknown drama, but they were completely oblivious of the tragedy. It was later that they discovered the truth of the horror that coincided with their arrival.

William Strachey, secretary of the new colony, gives the best detail of the event which, by the time he was writing in 1612, was already known to King James: 'his Majestie hath bene acquainted, that the men women, and Children of the first plantation at Roanoke were by practize and Commaundment of Powhatan (he himself perswaded thereunto by his Priests) miserably slaughtered without any offence given him . . . by the first planted (who 20. and od yeares had peaceably lived)'.[8]

Although the manner of informing James of Powhatan's treachery is not known – it may have been verbally or by document since lost – the further poof that the massacre had taken place is overwhelming. The instructions sent to Sir Thomas Gates, deputy Governor of the new colony from 1609 until the arrival of Lord De La Warr as first Governor, confirm Powhatan's slaughter of the lost colony. Captain John Smith, who later captured the affections of Pocahontas, Powhatan's daughter, and who, between 1608 and 1627, published five books on the Jamestown colony, was told of Powhatan's perfidy, probably by William White, a Jamestown colonist who lived amongst the Indians.[9] That Smith was aware of these events is confirmed by the Reverend Samuel Purchas, who attempted to carry on the history of English exploits where Hakluyt had left off. When publishing, in 1625, his book *Purchase his Pilgrimes,* he made the matter certain. Purchas inserted, 'Powhatan confessed to Cap. Smith that hee had been at their slaughter, and had divers utensils of theirs to show'.[10] The only evidence lacking is that of an eye-witness account.

This was no time to go looking for the lost colonists; the new colony had to be established. Nevertheless, the English soon found evidence that aliens had lived with the Indian tribes. On 8 May, when the new colonists had been at Chesapeake a bare twelve days, an exploring party travelled up the James River. They were some eighty miles from the sea when they were set upon by some heavily armed Indians equipped with, amongst other weapons, 'pieces of yron to cleave a man in sunder'.[11] The man who made this observation, George Percy, one of the gentlemen settlers, at an unidentifiable Indian village saw 'a Savage Boy about the age of ten yeeres, which had a head of haire of a perfect yellow and a reasonable white skinne, which is a Miracle amongst all Savages'.[12] Clearly George Percy connects both observations with the lost colony. It must not be forgotten, however, that by 1607 the foreign population of the area had been increased by others not of the lost colony; survivors from shipwrecks, wanderers from the French colony in the north and the Spanish colony in the south, as well as the considerable number of people of mixed race set free by Drake at Roanoke in June 1585.

By the end of 1607 Captain John Smith, an intrepid adventurer, had undertaken to explore a wide area and, in doing so, had been captured twice, once by Powhatan's brother and a second time by Powhatan himself. It was Powhatan's brother who told the captain of a group of men clothed like Smith only five days' journey distant – a statement confirmed by Powhatan later.[13] In January 1608, the month in which Christopher Newport returned from England bringing the first supplies, a search was organised for these men who wore European dress. But the chief who had offered guides became difficult and the searchers returned no wiser.

From his wide-ranging explorations Smith was able to produce a reasonable map of the area surrounding the Jamestown colony. The map, with notes, was sent to the Council of Virginia in London. Although the original map is lost, a copy has survived in the Archivo Central of Simancas in Spain, due entirely to the cunning of the Spanish ambassador in London, Don Pedro de Zuñiga, who was placed there to watch all that went on in England. Zuñiga intercepted Smith's map and had the copy made. On this map is marked, in the area of Cape Henry, 'here remayneth 4 men clothed that came from Roonock to Oconohowan'. The Council of Virginia in London responded to Smith's map and notes, including in their instruction to the Deputy Governor, Sir Thomas Gates, directions as to where to look for the four clothed men.

William Strachey, the secretary to the colony at Jamestown gives more detail of missing Roanoke colonists in his *Historie of Travell into Virginia Britania* of 1612. Commenting on the land lying to the south of the Jamestown settlement he wrote:

the People have howses built with stone walls, and one story above another, so taught them by those English who escaped the slaughter at *Roanock*, at what tyme this our Colony (under the conduct of Capt Newport) landed within the *Chesapeack Bay*, . . . and where at *Ritanoe*, the Wewroance *Eyanoco* preserved 7. of the English alive, fower men, twoo Boyes, and one young Maid, who escaped and fled up the River of *Choanoke*, to beat his Copper.[14]

Strachey is writing of something which took place about five years earlier and he is muddled about the site of the massacre when he tells us that it took place at Roanoke, an area outside Powhatan's domain. But clearly he had picked up a story of a group of Europeans living on the Chowan River.

Who was this small group of seven at Chawanoac, said to include two boys and a girl – if they existed at all. Did they rush blindly into the woods as they fled from Powhatan's slaughtering warriors, eventually finding their way to the Chowan River and following its course downstream? Were they perhaps the remnants of the fifteen left by Grenville in the fort at Roanoke in August 1586 – the fifteen who shortly became thirteen and then vanished off the Outer Banks? Had some of these thirteen found their way to Chawanoac and married Indian women? Or were they, perhaps, a group who had never been involved in the Powhatan massacre, but had been left at Chowan to man a staging post on the route to and from Roanoke – as outlined by Lane in his plans of 1585–6 for moving the colony to Chesapeake? We shall never know.

Smith certainly took their existence seriously and was not deterred by the failure of his first search party, sent out in January 1608. Early in 1609, he sent a man with two Indian guides to the Chowan River to look for the rumoured seven and to confirm if a certain type of grass suitable for textiles grew there. The grass grew all right, but for the seven there was 'little hope and lesse certaintie of them that were left by Sir Walter Rawley'.

That expedition was followed by another, ranging farther west into the mainland from the Chowan River. This, too, returned with no news of the settlers. Acting on the rumours he received, Smith can be said to have made some effort to search for Ralegh's lost colonists. How thorough his searchers were is another matter, given that they were in areas where the Indians were often hostile, were led by uncertain guides, and were grappling with an unfamiliar language.

It is not surprising that rumours lived on, echoing down the centuries, becoming more improbable as time went on. In the late nineteenth century, romantic attempts were made to show that the Lumbee Indians of North Carolina were descendants of the lost colonists: in 1891 Stephen Weeks ingeniously interpreted their quaint pronunciation of the language as being Old English. In 1881 Hamilton McMillan discovered that out of ninety-five surnames borne by the lost colonists forty-one coincided with Lumbee names.[15] Others pointed out that grey eyes and fair hair were sometimes found amongst the Lumbees. However, 300 years of exposure to English and European immigrants is sufficient to account for any un-Indian characteristics found amongst the tribe. In any group of 114 English, the chances of finding forty-one names resembling those of the colonists are high – their names were common enough. But some few colonists, certainly no more than a dozen at most – may have avoided the massacre.

The lost colony had, to all intents and purposes, disappeared by April 1607. The experience gained from those first settlers contributed to the success of the Jamestown settlement. It was one of history's pointless ironies that, as the first Jamestown settlers entered Chesapeake, the last of the Roanoke colonists were meeting their end. If Virginia Dare survived until then, she, and her follow colonists, died with the frightening sound of Indian war cries in their ears, pierced through by Indian arrows or beaten to death by the wooden clubs and stone–edged swords of Powhatan's men.

Appendix I

The Names of Lane's 1585 Colonists

The names of all those as well Gentlemen as others, that remained one whole yeere in Virginia, under the Government of Master Ralfe Lane.

Master Philip Amades,
    Admirall of the countrie
Master Hariot
Master Acton
Master Edward Stafford
Thomas Luddington
Master Marvyn
Master Gardyner
Captaine Vaughan
Master Kendall
Master Prideox
Robert Holecroft
Rise Courtney
Master Hugh Rogers
Thomas Foxe
Edward Nugent
Darby Glande
Edward Kelle
John Gostigo
Erasmus Clefs
Edward Ketcheman
John Linsey
Thomas Rottenbury
Roger Deane
John Harris
Frauncis Norris
Matthewe Lyne
Edward Kettell
Thomas Wisse

Master Thomas Harvie
Master Snelling
Master Anthony Russe
Master Allyne
Master Michel Polyson
John Cage
Thomas Parre
William Randes
Geffrey Churchman
William Farthowe
John Taylor
Philppe Robyns
Thomas Phillipes
Valentine Beale
James Skinner
George Eseven
John Chaundeler
Philip Blunt
Richard Poore
Robert Yong
Marmaduke Constable
Thomas Hesket
William Wasse
John Fever
Daniel
Thomas Taylor
Richard Humfrey
John Wright
Gabriell North

Robert Biscombe
William Backhouse
William White
Henry Potkin
Dennis Barnes
Joseph Borges
Doughan Gannes
William Tenche
Randall Latham
Thomas Hulme
Walter Myll
Richard Gilbert
Steven Pomarie
John Brocke
Bennet Harrye
James Stevenson
Charles Stevenson
Christopher Lowde
Jeremie Man
James Mason
David Salter
Richard Ireland
Thomas Bookener
William Philippes
Randall Mayne

Bennet Chappell
Richard Sare
James Lasie
Smolkin
Thomas Smart
Robert
John Evans
Roger Large
Humfrey Garden
Frauncis Whitton
Rowland Griffyn
William Millard
John Twyt
Edwarde Seklemore
John Anwike
Christopher Marshall
David Williams
Nicholas Swabber
Edward Chipping
Sylvester Beching
Vincent Cheyne
Haunce Walters
Edward Barecombe
Thomas Skevelabs
William Walters

The Names of the 1587 Virginia Colonists

'The names of all the men, women and Children, which safely arrived in Virginia, and remained to inhabite there, 1587.

Anno Regni Reginae Elizabethae. 29.

John White [Governor]
Roger Bailie [Assistant]
Ananias Dare [Assistant]
Christopher Cooper [Assistant]
Thomas Stevens [Assistant]
John Sampson [Assistant]
Dyonis Harvie [Assistant]
Roger Prat [Assistant]
George Howe [Assistant]
Simon Fernando [Assistant]

William Willes
John Brooke
Cutbert White
John Bright

Clement Tayler
William Sole
John Cotsmur
Humfrey Newton
Thomas Colman
Thomas Gramme

Nicholas Johnson
Thomas Warner
Anthony Cage
John Jones
John Tydway
Ambrose Viccars
Edmond English
Thomas Topan
Henry Berrye
Richard Berrye
John Spendlove
John Hemmington
Thomas Butler
Edward Powell
John Burden
James Hynde
Thomas Ellis
William Browne

Michael Myllet
Thomas Smith
Richard Kemme
Thomas Harris
Richard Taverner
John Earnest
Henry Johnson
John Starte
Richard Darige
William Lucas
Arnold Archard
John Wright
William Dutton
Morris Allen
William Waters
Richard Arthur
John Chapman
William Clement

Robert Little
Hugh Tayler
Richard Wildye
Lewes Wotton
Michael Bishop
Henry Browne

Marke Bennet
John Gibbes
John Stilman
Robert Wilkinson
Peter Little
John Wyles
Brian Wyles
George Martyn
Hugh Pattenson
Martyn Sutton
John Farre
John Bridger
Griffen Jones
Richard Shaberdge
James Lasie
John Cheven
Thomas Hewet
William Berde

Women
Elyoner Dare
Margery Harvie
Agnes Wood
Wenefrid Powell
Joyce Archard
Jane Jones
Elizabeth Glane
Jane Pierce
Audry Tappan
Alis Chapman
Emme Merrimoth
Colman
Margaret Lawrence
Joan Warren
Jane Mannering
Rose Payne
Elizabeth Viccars

Henry Rufoote
Richard Tomkins
Henry Dorrell
Charles Florrie
Henry Mylton

Henry Payne
Thomas Harris
William Nicholes
Thomas Phevens

John Borden
Thomas Scot

Savages
Manteo   That were in Englande
Towaye   and returned home into
         Virginia with them.

Boyes and Children
John Sampson
Robert Ellis
Ambrose Viccars
Thomas Archard
Thomas Humfrey
Tomas Smart
George Howe
John Prat
William Wythers

Children born in Virginia
Virginia Dare
Harvye

Appendix II: Lane's Fort on Roanoke Island

In choosing a site for the main fort Lane would have borne at least two essential points in mind: that it should defend the colony against an attack from the sea by way of the two inlets through the Banks, and that it should protect the settlement overlooking a harbour where the boats lay. The reconstructed Fort Raleigh site fails on both these points. Sited at the extreme north end of the island it leaves the channels into the Sound undefended, and the nearby Otis Cove, which provides a convincing but small harbour, is a comparatively modern natural development and was not there in 1585. Furthermore, the fort is far too small for the purpose of defending the main settlement. It was intended as a simple sconce to defend the northern end of Roanoke Island against a surprise attack by a seaborne enemy approaching from the north end of the Sound or the Albemarle River. Since it carried no cannons it could not have withstood a heavy attack.

Fort Raleigh is constructed in the form of a four-pointed star. It is of earth with bulwarks up to six feet high surrounded by a dry ditch five feet deep. The western, landward, point is taken up with an entrance, while the two points facing the Sound have platforms for swivel guns, and the fourth point, facing south towards the interior of the island, has no platform. Each exposed point is covered by a cavalier or 'spur' in the middle of the flanking bulwarks. It is a standard military construction recommended by contemporary theories on defence, whether for a city wall or small sconce. The only variation from the standard is that the bulwark on the landward south-east side is pierced by a secondary entrance which could be approached on foot only, to be used, no doubt, when the main entrance was blocked by a barricade. The greatest interior width from point to point is barely 100 feet and a large part of the centre was taken up by a hut, presumably for shelter.

Lane's fort was completed by 17 August – eighteen days after his arrival – and it must, by the time taken to build it, have been a much bigger affair than the present Fort Raleigh site, which would have taken a mere two or three days to throw up. Within its earth ramparts it would have been large enough to have taken, in an emergency, all the colonists with their precious stores and livestock. It would have been constructed on the standard star principle with platforms at each point for cannons. Around the inside of the ramparts there would have been a firing step to allow soldiers to shoot over the height of the six-feet-or-more ramparts protecting those within. Outside the fort would have been a deep protecting ditch. Within easy distance of the fort was the settlement which it protected. Trees and undergrowth would have been cleared from the area to give an open field of fire and to deprive attackers of cover.

A very thorough archaeological excavation of the Fort Raleigh site was carried out by J. C. Harrington at intervals between 1947 and 1953. No evidence of a settlement was uncovered and very few artifacts.* The latter fact indicates that Fort Raleigh was little used and we must look elsewhere for the site of Lane's bustling colony and his fort.

Three miles down the coast of Roanoke Island, to the south-east of the Fort Raleigh site, is Shallowbag Bay where the modern town of Manteo has grown up. The bay provides a sheltered harbour when gales whip the Sound up into dangerous turbulence. Furthermore, boats moored in the bay cannot be seen by prying eyes from the sea. In 1580-90 the marshland which now lies between Manteo town and Baum Point, around the north side of the bay, did not exist – it was dry land then – and Baum Point is the logical place for a defensive fort. A fort sited on or near Baum Point covers the entrance to Shallowbag Bay and both channels into the Sound, Port Ferdinando and Port Lane. With the colony settled on the shore of Shallowbag Bay, on what is now the marshy area, all the criteria required by Lane are fulfilled. Also the site satisfies the demands of Grenville and Grananimeo. Until the marshy ground is explored this must remain a matter of speculation. All that can be said with certainty is that the present Fort Raleigh was not the main fort. It is also time to say that any artifacts beneath the marsh will be perfectly preserved and can safely be left there.

* *Search for the Cittie of Ralegh,* by Jean Carl Harrington, Archeological Research Series Number Six, National Park Service, U.S. Department of the Interior, Washington, 1962.

Notes

1 'Neere to Heaven by Sea as by Land'

1 State Papers Domestic, Elizabeth 1, 12/126,49.
2 *Ibid.*, 12/175,95.
3 Bodleian Library, Oxford; Ashmole Ms. 487.
4 State Papers Domestic, Elizabeth 1, 12/149,66.
5 Richard Hakluyt, *Principall navigations,* London 1589, p. 695.

2 'Heathen and Barbarous Landes'

The quotations are taken from Arthur Barlow's discourse, or journal, of the 1584 voyage, first published in *Principal navigations* (P.N.) by Richard Hakluyt (1589), pp. 728–33; reprinted in *Roanoke Voyages* (R.V.) by D. B. Quinn, pp. 91–116.

1 D. B. Quinn, *England and the Discovery of America 1481–1620,* Allen & Unwin, London 1973, p. 255.
2 Irene A. Wright, *Further English Voyages to Spanish America,* Hakluyt Society, London 1951, pp. 175–6
3 Clifford M. Lewis, S.J., & Albert J. Loomie, S.J., *The Spanish Jesuit Mission in Virginia 1570–1582,* The University of North Carolina Press, Chapel Hill, 1953.

3 'The Empty Bay'

The principal source is the account based on the *Tiger's* journal, published in P.N. (1589), pp. 733–6; reprinted in R.V., pp. 178–93. Further details are from *Chronicles,* III, by Raphael Holinshed (1587), pp. 140–3; reprinted in R.V., pp. 173–8. Ralph Lane's account of the first colony was published in P.N. (1589), pp. 737–47; reprinted in R.V., pp. 255–94. Also from Thomas Hariot's *A Briefe and True Report,* first published in P.N. (1579), pp. 748–64; reprinted in R.V., pp. 317–387.

1 State Papers Domestic, James 1, vol xli, p. 119.
2 Elizabeth Donno (ed.), *An Elizabethan in 1582,* Hakluyt Society, London 1976, p. 221.

4 'The Manner of the Seas'

The same basic sources as previous chapter supplemented by the Spanish point of view taken from a report to Philip II, printed in R.V., pp. 733–8.

1 Wright, *op. cit.,* p. 9.
2 *Ibid.,* pp. 9–12.

5 'Trumpets and Consort of Music'

Same basic sources as previous chapter.
1 Wright, *op. cit.,* p. 16.
2 Quinn, *op. cit.,* pp. 269–75.

6 'Towne of Pomeiock'

Same basic sources as previous chapter.
1 Wright, *op. cit.,* pp. 174–6.

7 'Brick and Tiles for Fort and Houses'

Same basic sources as previous chapter supplemented by Derby Glande's comment taken from his interrogation by the Spanish authorities; printed in R.V., pp. 833–8.

8 'Port Ferdinando in Verginia'

Same basic sources as previous chapter supplemented by Ralph Lane's letters from Virginia (State Papers Colonial; Public Record Office, London); printed in R.V., pp. 197–214.
1 Sir Walter Raleigh, *The History of the World,* 1614, Book 1, pp. 175–6.
2 Essex Record Office, Ms. D/Drh,Mi.
3 Wright, *op cit.,* pp. 12–15.
4 The Azores, otherwise Portuguese, became subject to Spain in 1580-1604.

9 'Contrarie to all Expectation'

Same basic sources as previous chapter.
1 Ralph Lane uses the word 'Towne' for the settlement. This does not denote an urban street lay-out; he is using the word in the sixteenth century sense of settlement, evolved from the Saxon word *Tun* meaning farmstead.
2 William Strachey, *The History of Travell into Virginia Britania,* Louis B. Wright & Virginia Freund (eds.), Hakluyt Society, London 1953, p. 116. Here we are told that the wealthy tribesmen of Powhatan's time had more than one wife.

10 'A Camvisado'

Same basic sources as previous chapter.
1 The impression gained is that Lane was guarded possessively by his old Irish soldiers. His Irish boy winged the running Pemisapan, and Nugent, another Irishman, brought back the head. Perhaps they were associated with Lane in the Irish campaigns of 1583–5.

11 'Ankered all without the Harbour'

Same basic sources as previous chapter supplemented by details of Drake's voyage of 1586 from various sources, including the *Primrose* journal; all printed in R.V., pp. 294-311.

1 Julian S. Corbett (ed.), *Papers Relating to the Navy during the Spanish War 1585-1587*, Navy Records Society 1898, p. 10.

2 *Ibid.*, p. 11.

3 *Ibid.*, p. 24.

4 Wright, *op. cit.*, p. 199.

12 'A Wild Fire Arrow'

Same basic sources as previous chapter supplemented by John White's account of the 1587 Virginian voyage published in P.N. (1589), pp. 764-70; reprinted in R.V., pp. 515-43.

1 The contribution made by Ralegh's colonists to the history of tobacco was the introduction to England of clay pipes. J. C. Harrington, who excavated the Fort Raleigh site from 1951 to 1956 (*Search for the Cittie of Ralegh*, Archeological Research Series Number Six, National Park Service, U.S. Dept. of the Interior, Washington 1962), found both Indian and European clay pipes. Hariot noted the Indians' use of tabacco: 'they use to take the fume or smoke thereof by sucking it through pipes made of claie, into their stomacke and head; from whence it purgeth superfluous fleame and other grosse humors, openeth all pores and passages of the body'. After such a discovery it is not surprising that Hariot became a heavy pipe smoker.

Likewise the potato was not introduced into England by Ralegh. The only edible roots which Hariot reported were the ground-nut, mash-potato, the root of the wild potato vine and the duck potato. John Gerard in his *Herball* of 1597 invented the name 'Virginian Potato' (Solanium Tuberosum), which was not growing in Virginia in Hariot's time.

13 'The Fort Raised Down'

Uses the same account by John White as the previous chapter.

1 A. L. Rowse, *Sir Richard Grenville of the Revenge*, Jonathan Cape, London 1940, p. 249.

2 William S. Powell, *Roanoke Colonists and Explorers: An Attempt at Identification*, North Carolina Review, xxxiv, 1957.

3 John White's account of the old settlement is the clearest description given, and it poses problems. White is the only witness to put the fort at the north end of the island. He was, however, a slipshod reporter and he could have intended to convey that they 'walked to[wards] the North Ende of the Island'. White goes on to say that there were dwelling houses about the fort. Yet none has been discovered in the archaeological digs carried out by J. C. Harrington at Fort Raleigh. Moreover, for a site occupied for two periods of many months each, too few artifacts have been discovered at Fort Raleigh.

14 *'Children Born in Virginia'*

Uses the same account by John White as the previous chapter.

15 *'Not a Little Distressed'*

John White's account of the voyage of the *Brave* and the *Roe* was first published in P.N. (1589), pp. 771–3; reprinted in R.V., pp. 562–9. Alonso Ruiz's account is published in R.V. pp. 781–4.

1 Rowse, *op. cit.*, p. 259.

16 *'Anciente Silke'*

The principal source of the attempt to relieve the colony in 1590 is taken from John White's narrative first published in P.N., vol. 111 (1600), pp. 288–95; reprinted in R.V., pp. 598-622.

17 *'Where our Planters were Left'*

Uses the same principal source as the previous chapter.

1 Quinn, *op. cit.*, p. 446.

18 *'A Whole Country of English'*

1 Quinn, *op. cit.*, p. 278.
2 *Ibid.*, p. 405.
3 *Ibid.*, pp. 419–31.
4 *Ibid.*, p. 428.
5 Philip L. Barbour, *The Jamestown Voyages Under the First Charter 1606–1609*, Hakluyt Society, London 1969, p. 134.
6 Strachey, *op. cit.*, p. 104.
7 Barbour, *op. cit.*, p. 134.
8 Strachey, *op. cit.*, p. 91.
9 Quinn, *op. cit.*, p. 467.
10 Samuel Purchase, *Hakluytus posthumus or Purchase his Pilgrimes* (4 vols), London 1626; reprinted (20 vols) Hakluyt Society, extra series xiv-xxxii, Glasgow 1905–07, vol. 19, pp. 227-8.
11 Barbour, *op. cit.*, p. 138.
12 *Ibid.*, p. 140.
13 *Ibid.*, p. 182.
14 Strachey, *op. cit.*, p. 34.
15 Stephen B. Weeks, *The Lost Colony of Roanoke: Its Fate and Survival*, Papers of the American Historical Association, Vol 5, Part 4, (1691) 107–146. Hamilton McMillan, *Sir Walter Raleigh's Lost Colony*, Raleigh, N.C.; Edwards and Broughton Company, 1888.

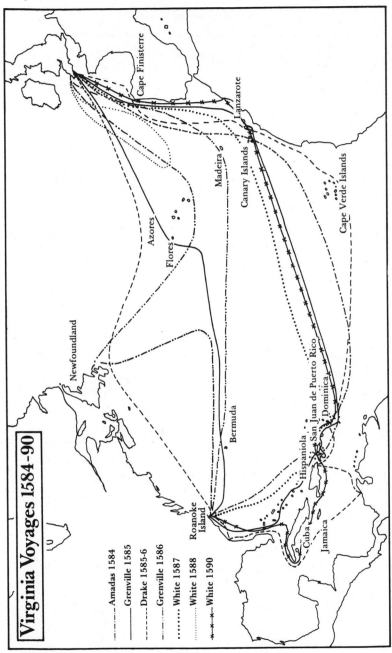

Virginia Voyages 1584-90

Cape Finisterre

Lanzarote

Madeira

Canary Islands

Cape Verde Islands

Azores

Flores

Newfoundland

Bermuda

Hispaniola

San Juan de Puerto Rico

Dominica

Roanoke Island

Cuba

Jamaica

- - - · - Amadas 1584
———— Grenville 1585
- - - - Drake 1585-6
- · - · - Grenville 1586
· · · · · · · White 1587
· · · · · · White 1588
—×—×— White 1590

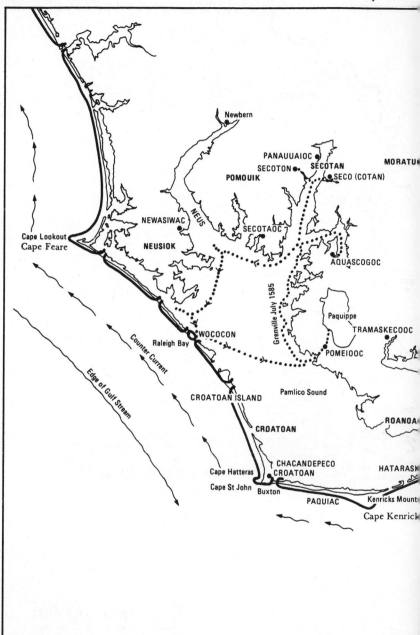

Newbern

PANAUUAIOC ●
SECOTON ●— ● **SECOTAN**   **MORATU**
POMOUIK   ● SECO (COTAN)

NEWASIWAC ●   SECOTAOC ●

NEUS

NEUSIOK

Cape Lookout
Cape Feare

AQUASCOGOC ●

Grenville July 1585

Paquippe
TRAMASKECOOC ●

WOCOCON
Raleigh Bay

POMEIOOC ●

Counter Current

Pamlico Sound

Edge of Gulf Stream

CROATOAN ISLAND

CROATOAN

ROANOA

CHACANDEPECO
Cape Hatteras   **CROATOAN**
Cape St John   Buxton   HATARASK

PAQUIAC   Kenricks Mount

Cape Kenrick

POWHATAN CONFEDERACY

MANGOAK

MORATUC

●RAMUSHONNOUK

CHAWANOAC

OPOSSIAN

Williamsburg ●

MORATUC
Plymouth
TANDAQUOMUC
OHANOAK CHAWANOAC

METACKWEM

TRIPANICK

Lane's Projected Route 1586

WAROWTANI

James River

WEAPEMEOC

WEAPEMEOC

Dismal Swamp

Newport News

MEQUOPEN

CAUTAKING

Elizabeth City

RICKAHOKENE

Norfolk

SKICOAK

CHEPANOC

CHESEPIAN

APASUS

Chesapeake Bay

PASQUENOKE

CHESEPIUC

Cape Henry

Chesapeake Expedition 1585-6

Durant Island

DASEMUNKEPEUC

ROANOAC

Manteo
Bodie Island
Port Lane
Roanoke Island
Port Ferdinando

Counter Current

N

0 1 2 3 4 5
Scale of Miles

ATLANTIC OCEAN

●●●●●●● Grenville 1585
───── Lane 1586
━ ━ ━ ━ Chesapeake Bay Expedition 1585-6
Estimated coast line in 16th century
Indian Towns:— POMEIOOC
Indian Tribe Lands:— SECOTAN
Elizabethan names:— Cape Kenrick

Virginia 1584-90

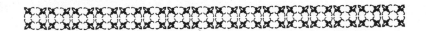

Index

A resident of Bleasby, in Nottinghamshire, England, David Durant is the author of two historical biographies, *Bess of Hardwick,* and *Arbella Stuart.* He has contributed to *Country Life* and *History Today* in Britain, and spends part of each year in the United States, where he lectures and conducts research.

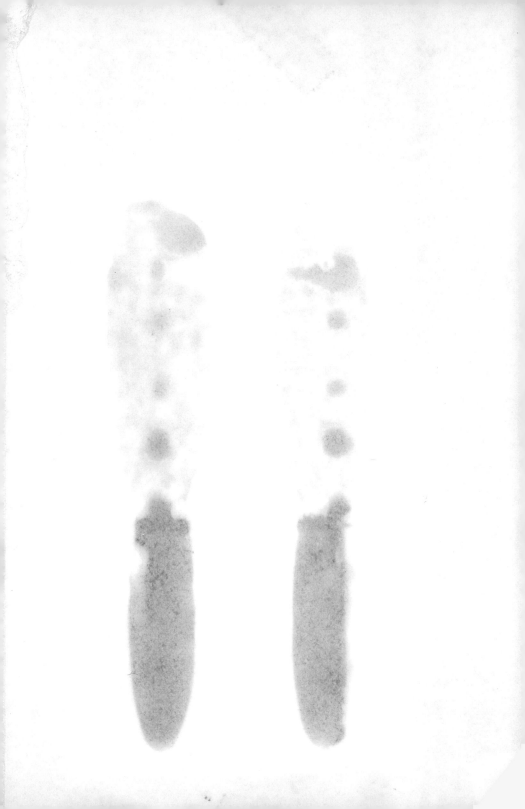

Ralegh's lost colony.